Set Sail

Shine Your Radiance
Activate Your Ascension
Ignite Your Income
Live Your Legacy

Essays from 20 New Feminine Evolutionaries
Featuring **Alis Mao, Ari Haff, Dr. Rima Bonario, & Windy Cook**
Compiled by Jane Astara Ashley

FLOWER *of* LIFE PRESS

Praise

"In Ari's essay 'Path of the Priestess', surrender and trust are absolutely founda-tional. The mind simply cannot carry you where you are intending to travel on this path. Ari offers a beautiful form of transport in that journey through a personal Witness of the soul journey into fully embodying that knowing as a living reality rather than a mental concept. She offers hope and clear direction to those who are still growing into the full embodiment of trust and surrender and discovering the passion of their soul path."

—Ariel Spilsbury, Founder of the 13 Moon Mystery School and scribe of the Source material for that school, Author of The 13 Moon Oracle: Holographic Meditations on the Mystery

"'A New Bloom: Navigating the Alchemy of Life' by Faye Callaway is an absolutely beautiful piece. It is eloquently written and captivated me immediately. I have not felt so inspired in a long time."

—Mercedes Heater

"Rima Bonario has a way with words that cuts right to the center of my being. Every word seems perfectly chosen to express just what I need to read. As I read her work, I find tears flowing. Tears of recognition of authentic truth. This work is a blessing to anyone who will receive it."

—Rev. Elizabeth Mora, M.Div., Unity Northwest Church

"Jamie Brandenburg is a talented, intuitive healer who is instrumental in bringing people together to support one another on their healing journeys, and most import-ant, inspiring the greatest journey within the self to be a greater contribution to the world. Her excerpt in the book Set Sail, 'The Illumination of Your Divine Self' is an enlightening and thorough, step-by-step guide to igniting the most beautiful light inside of you, from new beginnings to creating sacred rituals to inspiring greater connection to your highest, most powerful and beautiful self. Very inspiring! I encourage you to download her free gift as well—everyone could use more grounding and protection to call in our sacred space. Breathtaking."

—Bridget Cook-Burch, New York Times Bestselling Author

"Lara's story is an insightful, powerful, beautiful story of 'mirror-like wisdom'—using the adversities in life to reflect the areas within us that still need healing. Wonderfully mature and beautifully written, demonstrating exceptional insight and wisdom."

—Devi Ward Erickson, Founder of The Institute of Authentic Tantra Education & Creator of Authentic Tantra®

"*Karina Mountain Bluebird's story calls us into an adventure of spirit with her as she takes a series of wild leaps of faith, trusting the mystery of her intuitive guidance. Her chapter sounds a bold call to the reader to return to the path of the sacred feminine and join her as a wild, free, elemental honoring, heart-connected woman who listens to the signs and reads the symbols on her heroine's journey. I was inspired to feel Karina boldly leading the way, stepping into her mythic story as a shaman. She who is summoned by spirit...she who perseveres beyond worldly obstacles...she who remembers miracles happen when we are in alignment with our souls.*"

—Eden Amadora, Women's empowerment coach,
Priestess of the 13 Moon Mystery school

"*In Set Sail, Dr. Davia Shepherd tells all in her soft, strong voice. Her generous physical spirit and emotional grit comes through loud and clear; she wants for her patients what she has done for herself: to enjoy the best quality of life based on good health. She wants to spare the reader the trauma of her lesson learned: a person cannot be their best without self-care. She goes back to her core and shares how she rebuilt her foundation to fend off illness and embrace her best current and future self. A quick read for a momentous inspiration!*"

—Leslie Gold McPadden, LGM Injury Law

"*In Set Sail, Mary Tan points us in the direction of spiritual ascension. If anyone feels lost or at a loss, you will understand through these wise and channeled words written from the heart and experience of someone who walks the path. Take her hand and read this amazing book. I promise you will feel more at peace and assured in your heart. It will help you stop questioning your existence and start your way to love and ascension while experiencing an expanded dimension in life.*"

—Sarah Baez, Spirit Quest Productions

"*In the book Set Sail, Nicole Olthoorn's words say so much more than what she has written on paper. I recognize a lot of myself in it and I am sure it will attract many other readers who have some form of resistance towards claiming their own power, too. You have to be ready to read this. For this is not just a chapter in a book, it's a call to fully unleash yourself.*"

—Tanja Zieverink

"Alisa's beautiful real-life story shows that no matter how lost we may feel or how stuck things might seem, there is an undeniable force shaping our lives, taking us exactly back to who we actually are. Her words remind me that the journey is all about manifesting the unique love that we are. I can't wait to visit her healing farm!"

—Catalina Rivera Dois, Feminine Mysteries Mentor,
Blood Mysteries Keeper

"What strikes me about Allecia's writing is that it emanates from her heartfelt experience. Those who have had a profound experience of 'knowing' with an animal will recognize the truth in Allecia's experience and the call to work with animals in a true way. Communication with animals is not something most people set out to do, but it evolves in some people as they become open vessels to hear what animals have to say, through actions, words, and moments like Allecia describes in Set Sail. If the other contributions to this collection are as honest and engaging as Allecia's, then it will be a valuable read for those who are interested in exploring the world of animal 'commune-ication.'"

—Susan Smith, Founder of Equine Body Balance

"DaniElle Ashé gives a heartfelt window into the true paradoxical nature behind living your dream—the pain and discomfort that accompanies the beauty and contentment of a life truly lived. She is brave in her honesty and determination to lead with her heart, and I find in her words inspiration to follow the deep call of the Divine within."

—Susan Marasul, VEOArts

"Lara Wynn's story 'A Beautiful Mess' is riveting in authentic disclosure. Her transparency in sharing her very personal and poignant journey illuminates an evolving paradigm on the luminous nature of love. She forms a bridge from archaic social conditioning into a new exemplification of conscious loving relationships that are possible for us all. Her sacred work guides others in releasing trauma, guilt, and shame, then gently leads them into deeper intimacy within their own heart."

—Daria Kathleen Sherman PhD, Author

"I am viscerally struck by the potency of a transmission so authentic and embodied it begins to thaw and heal frozen places in me just in the reading of it. The truth of this story, of Dana Schlick's inner alchemy and experience, ripples out as an offering...as an initiation, as an invitation and companion towards our own journey of transformation and reclamation of the fullness of who we are. It illuminates a pathway of integration and healing, of how we too can weave the pleasure and pain of our own experience into a beautiful creation of life. We are blessed by her willingness to dive so deep into her own process and embodiment. We are blessed by her desire to share her story and by the offerings of healing and support that she provides for the community through one-on-one sessions and group ritual work."

—Gitanjali Hemp, SyntaraSystem.com

"Set Sail crossed my path at a moment when I needed it most. Adrianne Spirallight's chapter, 'Easy Joy: Remembering the More of Who We Are', popped open with a burst of light, reconnecting tattered threads of remembrance, reminding me of things I had lost track of or forgotten. At a time when it's so easy to feel lost or astray, essays like this are a balm for the world-weary soul. For those of us on a spiritual path—named or not—it's easy to go adrift in these big storms. This book provides deep compassionate Wisdom and tools anchored in Hope and Truth that can set you back on your soul course. I adore what's in these pages."

—Claire Sierra, MA, LFT, Author The Magdalene Path

"In this wonderful offering in Set Sail, Ari Haff takes a journey of discovery into what it really means to trust in the magic, mystery and miracles of life. As a dyed in the wool scientist, Ari shares her own struggle to 'let go of having to know' in order to embrace the magic of 'not knowing' and in so doing, let the great unexpected joys of being fully present in her in life unfold. You will no doubt find yourself mirrored in this heartfelt, honest and deeply human story of remembrance and the joy of coming home to just how often miracles are waiting to be felt and seen in our everyday lives—if we would just stop trying to plan them away! Enjoy the ride with Ari as your guide!"

—Elayne Kalila Doughty MA, MFT, Ordained Priestess,
Psychotherapist, Sacred Ecstatic Activist, Gatekeeper and
Focalizer of the Priestess Presence Temple

"'Communion with the Animals' is so beautifully written, captivating and so sweetly open and inviting that I feel Allecia Evan's words and experience within my being awakening my own remembering. I have always felt the love and deep connection—that communion with all of nature—but never thought that it could be precognitive or many of its other gifts. You've taught me to look deeper, for greater gifts, awarenesses, and awakenings...for a richer, more connected communion."

—Sherry Quernstrom, Author of Shine

Are You Ready To Be A Published Author?

Books are the best business card you can have, whether you are an entrepreneur building your company, or a changemaker with a message that needs to be heard. Flower of Life Press is committed to giving voice to authors—and offering the support that is critical to birthing an authentic and powerful book.

We are ready to serve you with writing coaching, editing, and design while we provide the marketing team that will propel your journey and electrify your audience!

Check us out now at **floweroflifepress.com**—and have your book published by the team with over 3,000 books to their credit!

FLOWER *of* LIFE PRESS

Set Sail: Shine Your Radiance, Activate Your Ascension, Ignite Your Income, Live Your Legacy

Copyright © 2019 Flower of Life Press

The content of this book is for general instruction only. Each person's physical, emotional, and spiritual condition is unique. The instruction in this book is not intended to replace or interrupt the reader's relationship with a physician or other mental health professional. Please consult your doctor for matters pertaining to your specific health.

Cover and Book design by Jane Ashley, floweroflifepress.com
To contact the publisher, visit floweroflifepress.com

Library of Congress Control Number: 2019912354
Flower of Life Press, Old Saybrook, CT.

ISBN 978-1-7337409-6-8

Printed in the United States of America

"*I am not afraid of storms, for I am l
earning how to sail my ship.*"

—Louisa May Alcott

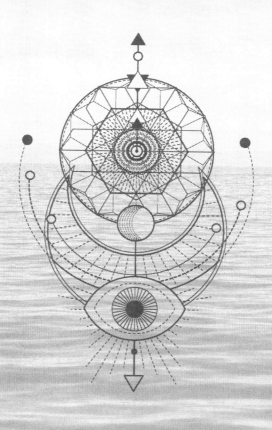

Contents

Introduction

by Jane Astara Ashley,
Publisher, Flower of Life Press

Set Sail, Set Sail...into the vastness of your power.

Five years ago my world shifted—like tectonic plates grindingly moving towards a new age, my journey hadn't been quick, and a lot of rocky barriers had been smashed along the way. Everything was moving more quickly, and my circle of sisters was feeling it, too... My balance was tilting me towards something special, different, scary... I was evolving, elevating from one resonant field to another, and it wasn't a smooth transition. I kept bumping into my limiting beliefs; about money, power, and my own self-worth, negative energy fighting to hold me back from the fresh field of potential and challenge suddenly alight in my grid. I was frazzled—and when I drove my car into a huge tree about 200 yards from my house, I knew that Spirit was giving me a BIG wake up call!

As always, it was my sisters who supported me, guided me through the dark night, and showed me the way towards my next chapter—defining, nurturing, and energizing the New Feminine Evolutionary!

My vision of the new woman began with a bubbling pool of primordial ooze...bright moonlight illuminating the emergence of a feminine form, rising from the muck, shedding the chains of patriarchy and centuries of servitude with each step forward. Suddenly, I understood evolution as a process happening now! Right before my eyes: courageous beings stepping forward, confronting this New Age with sword, shield, and an open heart—leaders who needed a forum to deepen into the conversation and provide guidance to the expanding community.

After four successful books in this series, my own evolution has led me to an exciting place, another opportunity to embark on the journey of elevation. I'm ready to find new pastures to thrive in, and the amazing authors within these pages are, too.

So you may be wondering what "Set Sail" really means... As a metaphor, I love the sense of presence this title carry—a vibration of awareness and anticipation. When I close my eyes, I feel the sun on my face, and the soft breeze caressing my skin—and the exciting energy awakening me to the journey ahead. I am here NOW. Ready to say "Yes" to whatever is next!

The word "Sail" is also an acronym:

"S" stands for *Shine!* Your radiance is all about activating your inner light. When we face the inevitable darkness, we must expand our capacity to receive light in our energy bodies in order to transmute and alchemize all lower energies and vibrations. We must continually "tune" our vessel to be able to receive and transmit information. Embodying the Divine is a joy, and a responsibility: it is our obligation to be able to clear out anything that would dim our light, so we can resonate with love. This kind of Radiance is not about exterior beauty; it's about open hearts, and our ability to love ourselves as well as each other in a way that is pure and unconditional—without judgment and without censoring ourselves.

"A" stands for *Activate Your Ascension.* *Activate* is easy to understand: Light your fire! Ignite your destiny! Find your spark! Stagnation is not an option, sister! The Universal Law of Action is clear: you must do the things and perform the actions necessary to achieve what you are setting out to do. Unless you take actions that are in harmony with your thoughts and dreams and proceed in an orderly fashion towards what you want to accomplish, there will be absolutely no foreseeable results. *Action* is imperative. You must act!

Every step leads you towards the other "A"...*Ascension.* In my world, evolution has been happening powerfully for the past ten years, ever since I burned down my former life and belief systems. Believe me, it hasn't *felt* much like ascension—I had to unlearn EVERYTHING I ever believed in and clear a seemingly endless series of program loops.

Only after the really tough work could I begin to create new beliefs and new thoughts that serve the ALL ONENESS (not just my ego) and serve our ascension into a higher frequency. When we ascend, our old attachments drop away as our frequency shifts into a new bandwidth. We must *let go*—this letting go is the juicy part of what *Set Sail* is all about! If you are on the shore, gazing at the vast expanse of the sea, ready to hop on your boat, there's quite a bit of fear and unknown in that situation—and you must leave all your baggage on shore. The waves can be stormy or the water smooth as glass—sometimes terrifying and cleansing all at the same time. Light and dark await this part of your quest. The leap from the known into the unknown is at the heart of the *Set Sail* message.

"I" is all about *igniting your income!* Money is energy and is just one fractal of what I'm talking about... Mama Earth is a cornucopia of lush abundance, and it's all at your disposal if you open to receive it. Your responsibility is to fulfill your role as a conscious and evolving woman, engaging with your family and community from a place of love and empathy and giving and serving without judgment or selfishness. When you are working with good intention in a non-harming profession, and striving for solutions instead of creating problems, then you will find yourself in the flow of abundance and will be fully resourced to continue creating...because no one can serve from depletion! You will be rewarded with the same high-vibrations you created with your resonance, and if you have taken right action, money will be the currency of Universal Flow—as well as many other gifts. In order for all of this energy to flow unimpeded, you must be ready to receive—confident, sovereign, and ready to embrace abundance without fear or guilt.

It took a bankruptcy a few years ago for me to realize how totally messed up I was with money—and that opened the door to other blocks and negative energy around my self-worth, deeply-ingrained scarcity, and blasé acceptance of being undervalued and underpaid. I knew I needed to relearn everything I knew about exchange: What it *really* is, why I was not receiving what I "deserved," and what steps did I need to take in order to elevate out of the state of malaise that seemed to take the joy out of everything. I'd been burning the candle at both ends for years, doing deep, meaningful work with amazing women, midwifing books out into the world, and supporting the voices of change-makers and visionaries. But I was under-resourced, undercharging, and undervaluing my services and my gifts.

Igniting my own income has required valuing myself so that I can charge what I'm worth, receive gratefully, and share my gifts with the world—a *win-win!* My intention has been to create a new relationship with Universal flow, an infinite exchange that starts internally, when we understand that we are the cause for any effect we see in our lives; when I take radical responsibility for everything that I've created (the good, the bad, and the ugly) and open myself to truth without fear, shame, or guilt, only then can I receive the gifts of my creation. Money is just one *effect* of our creations—abundance, love, relationships, intimacy, joy, and enlightenment are also effects of our creative power. I wasn't ready to "set sail" until I had released all negative thoughts about money and reprogrammed my unwillingness to receive abundance with a clear conscience and a commitment to serve others with ample resources and transformative energy.

Finally, "L" is for *Live Your Legacy.* There's no time like the present. Your presence on the planet at this time is required. What are you doing today to live your legacy? How are you serving the world on your path? It's wonderful to leave a story of success after your transition, but people need support, community, and leadership NOW. I love books because not only do they make an immediate impact, but the words and resonance carry on *forever.*

The book in your hands captures the power of life, death, and rebirth. Transformation and evolution is an on-going journey, with no finish line, nowhere to get to, nowhere to be other than right where you are in each moment. So why not enjoy the ride and say YES to all of it?

So, sisters and brothers, please read on to experience the magic and wisdom from these wonderful authors who have gathered together to weave many voices into ONE voice of love and transformation. Take your time with each chapter. Skip around as you wish.

Embrace your freedom and embark on your greatest journey...setting sail on a great adventure—the chance of a lifetime! Exciting and scary all at once, like a remembrance from the past and an urging from the future that whispers,

"Say yes, beloved...step forward...now is the time to let go of the baggage and cut the ropes! Your future is up to you...Set Sail into the vast expanse of your Shining Radiance, Ascension, Income, and Legacy."

Happy sailing!

Love, Astara

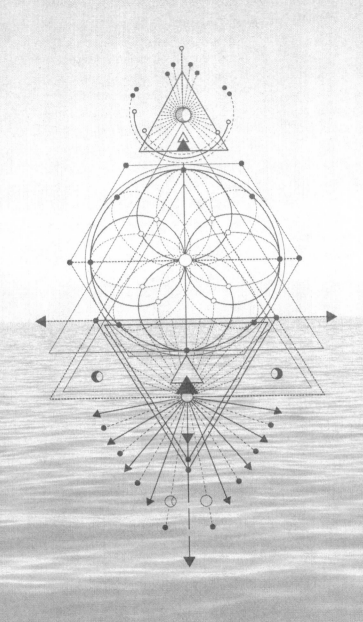

Safe Harbor

BY ALIS MAO

As I reflect on my own life and how I have surrendered and placed my trust in God, this scene from the film *Titanic* resonates with me:

> *Rose carefully steps out to the very edge and to the front of the ship as Jack assures her with these powerful words, "Trust me, Rose." She trusts Jack as she stands at the railing. He holds her arms gently and extends them out to the sides, like wings, as Rose says, "I'm flying!"*

Rose was able to truly feel alive once she surrendered and trusted. And through my own surrender, the universe has lit my path and led me to safe harbor.

> *"He will cover you with his feathers, and under his wings you will find refuge; his faithfulness will be your shield and rampart."*
>
> —Psalm 91:4

As a single mother of two young men, one in college and the other following not too far behind, I have ridden the rough waves of life with these two amazing souls. There were plenty of times when I questioned my abilities as a mother and second-guessed my choices.

Will my chosen partner accept and love my children as his own?
Will my children be accepting of the person I choose to be with?

I tread lightly when making decisions, being mindful of the effect on my children. Wearing both the mom and dad hats raising my boys wore on me. I would shed tears, praying my parenting skills were enough to raise two wonderful men. But when I surrender and pour all my trust out to the universe, I find I am always guided and steered in the right direction and I am reminded that I am doing my best. My boys affirm this with their loving hugs and little compliments. My children have been my biggest comforter and supporter along the path of life's challenges. They have cried with me, laughed with me, cheered with me, and nudged me to keep moving onward and upward. They return to me elements I have given to them in life. I know they are always under God's wings and are safe and protected.

I had to make hard decisions along the way, and one of the biggest decisions as of late was to walk away from a life of financial comfort working with a real estate team composed of eight strong-minded people—all men, other than myself. We had worked together for more than nine years, but over time I became numb and found myself just going through the motions. I was losing my soul spark—and my health. The universe could feel my energy radiating sadness, fear, pain, and a slow internal death. I took a leap of faith and decided to go out and show homes to a buyer. I was so determined to remind myself I was capable of doing the job on my own and wouldn't need to sit in a cubicle, feeling caged.

I closed the real estate transaction. However, I fell down a flight of stairs twice before closing the deal and continued to work without time off to recover. God and the universe heard my prayers and heart yearning for time off to heal and refresh my energy and focus on self-care. There is a saying that says to be careful of what you pray or wish for because it will be answered, but not always as you had wished. Because of those falls, I suffered a concussion and excruciating pain. And I realized that no one would take care of me and my health without me making my health a priority. The message came as confirmation for me to make that decision to no longer be with the team.

I received a message from a team member's daughter who spoke her truth in anger, sharing her thoughts of other people's perceptions and rumors of my lack of work ethic within the team. For me, this was the straw that broke the camel's back. I had raised her since she was four years old, and she was like a daughter to me! She told me that if I didn't work there anymore, everything would work out. Her words ignited in my heart. I had always given my all, but, no matter how much effort I put forth, it was never enough.

All this made me question myself, my abilities, and my capabilities. Not only did I feel excruciating pain all over my body with constant nausea from the falls, but I was falling into deep depression.

I broke down and spoke with my boys about my decision. I wanted their blessing and didn't want their hearts to have any resistance to the change in life I was about to announce. My heart was pounding, fear was my constant companion, and the unknown became my reality at that instance.

My boys were so supportive, more so than I had expected. Kyle said, "Mom, you keep repeating you're not happy and want to leave, but you keep going back. Make a decision and do it." Cody said, "Mom, go and be happy. You always tell us to find our happiness. Life is a journey and should be lived with amazing experiences. Kick fear in the ass and go adventure. What you fear most, will be the most rewarding."

I stopped going to work. My income lessened and, within months, I had exhausted my savings and was living on borrowed funds from my kids' savings. My depression grew, and I found myself without an ounce of motivation. I felt lifeless. My thoughts and ideas of how to create financial flow became very blurry. I cried a river of tears.

Because I had a real estate license, I considered continuing in that field, but my heart felt drained simply by the thought of it. I also wanted to avoid 9-to-5 jobs so I could be more available for my children. But, as I pondered, bills piled up. My energy level dipped, and I felt utterly depleted. So I put my pride aside and asked for help. Normally, I was more comfortable being the giver. I would give without reservation to family and strangers alike, never asking for anything in return. I just knew in my heart that whatever abundance the universe provided for me; I would share it with others. But this time, I needed assistance and felt the shame and embarrassment of it. I felt like I was starting over. My brother came to my rescue and paid my bills, and I was truly grateful. However, my loans were beginning to accrue.

I had filed for bankruptcy five years earlier and had worked for five years to restore my credit. With that card already played, I just felt hopeless. But I did what my heart knew to do and continued praying for the rough waves to shift so I wouldn't continue to drown. I prayed for a windfall.

Then I received a call from my cousin Sophia, who let me know that my auntie in Australia was very sick and had been diagnosed with stage 4 ovarian cancer. She requested that my mom and I travel to be with the family. The last time I remembered seeing my auntie and that side of the family was more than thirty-five years earlier. We had all departed from the refugee camp in Thailand, going our separate ways to different sponsors all around the world. I never understood my family tree and how I was to call this ninety-year-old woman my aunt. And, financially, this was bad timing for me.

Sophia messaged me again, saying that auntie kept repeating my father's name *Mao Bunthan* and she swore he was alive and came to her every day. Thus, my curiosity heightened, and my heart yearned to be there with auntie and that side of the family. I was curious to hear her life story. I wanted to understand and connect the dots.

I had been writing an inspirational memoir called "Garden of Hope," of my journey to find my biological father, Mao Bunthan, whom I had never met. He was very well known and had millions of beloved fans in Cambodia. My dad was a five-star commander in Cambodia and was sent to report to King Sihanouk and Prime Minister La Nol. His role was to represent the citizens and also to protect the king. My father was loved by the King and thus was adopted as his son and became his family. Over time, his appearance on the radio and television reporting for the King made him a beloved public figure. He saw the opportunity to serve the people of Cambodia and wanted to give Kampuchea people love, laughter, and hope in the midst of the gruesome Cambodian War. He composed music for the famous singer Sin Sisamouth and wrote television scripts for actors and actresses. He even included himself in some of the shows! In my interviews with his fans worldwide, they all honor him as a selfless man of deep compassion who saved millions of lives through his writing and humbleness. He traded his own life to save others in the infamous Cambodian War known as the "Killing Fields."

While I was in Australia, my auntie told me that she was my biological father's older sister. They were the closest of the four siblings. Her six surviving children of twelve shared that her dementia comes and goes, but her memory of my father was clear as crystal. She and I sat for hours together one night when everyone else in the house went on an outing. As I rubbed her swollen feet, auntie took me with her down memory lane. Her stories were so vivid, as if she were reliving each moment in the present and I was simply along for the ride. Her children later confirmed all were truths. I loved every moment spent with her. It was as if I was seeing my father through her eyes and heart. It was as if he was indeed alive...I felt his presence with us during those moments.

My heart was grateful that the Australia travel occurred. It was needed for that chapter of my life. Little did I know another trip was soon to take place that would change the course of my life entirely. My next travel adventure would serve as an important reminder from the universe about something that I had forgotten and had instead replaced with stress and fear.

My blessing came two weeks later from the Australia travel agent. This trip was fully paid for by a divine soul. My next destination: Peru! But this time, fear snuck on the trip with me. My best friend Tammie reminded me I needed this trip and hinted that I would experience an epiphany while in Peru.

In the air prior to landing in Cusco, Peru, the buildings and houses seemed as if an earthquake had just hit and destroyed them all. Everything looked unfinished and ruined. Stepping out from the airport, I embraced the warm sunshine, which my body craved after the continuous Oregon rain. I felt like I was pulled back in time one thousand years.

We were greeted by our tour guide, David, who arranged everything for us for the rest of our stay. He assigned Jose to be our personal tour guide. Little did we know we would bond with him and call him our newfound friend.

We began our journey anchored at the foot of Machu Picchu. The next morning, rising early, we were bused to the world-famous Machu Picchu ruins. The locals and every tour guide assured us that it would rain hard that day. Everyone had a poncho on or was buying one. But not me. I was sure God would bless us with sunshine and reveal Machu Picchu's beauty. We all smiled and prayed for sunshine.

God must have heard my prayer that day because Machu was more than breathtaking! I immersed myself in its eight-hundred-year-old wisdom, deep Mother Nature love, and timeless history resting at about 8,000 feet in elevation. Later, as we wished Machu farewell, our hearts felt sadness and we wondered when we would unite again. Our train whistled its gentle chorus as we sat inside on comfortable seats waiting to arrive at our next destination.

Our tour guide Jose met us at the train station and drove us to many more magnificent sites. Each place held its own precious history and spiritual beauty. Along the path to each destination, we were blessed with picturesque landscapes that filled us with wonder and awe. One of the hardest but most rewarding hikes I experienced had to be Rainbow Mountain, or Montina de Colores, at an elevation of 17,060 feet. Once again, we were told it would rain. Jose winked at me and told the locals that the weather had been only pure miracles for us. Jose reserved horses for us to ride up to the foot of the mountain, but we chose to only ride for a couple of minutes up for the experience. We hiked our way up while taking brief rests to catch our breath, all the while taking in the magnificent Andes Mountain peeking at us with its amazing beauty. I believe that was my distraction and saving grace to make it to the foot of the mountain. My heart screamed a sigh of hope when I heard echoes of celebration from other tourists who had hiked up before us made it to the top. As the climb grew higher, the cold air numbed my hands and my oxygen became scarce. I could hear my heart beating like a drum and my head spinning. Many times, I yearned to give up. But I glanced over to the Peruvian women and men who walked alongside their horses, ridden by tourists. These people made their way up and down the mountain on a muddy trail without fear, doubt, or complaint, every day, making the climb look so easy, smiling with gratitude. I continued on.

To my right, I saw vibrant colors of the incredible mountains: aqua, maroon, red, purple, blue... It looked as if someone had taken a brush and painted them.

I still had a way to go to get to the top! *I can do this!* I saw people sliding at the edge as they climbed down from the top. It made my hands clammy and my heart fill with fear as I imagined falling down and off the edge. I made sure to stay in the middle, and practically crawled up. I saw clear quartz crystals growing in with the rainbow rocks and I felt their safe aura. (I love crystals and my house is full of them.) The wind blew strong with frost against my face and hands. Heaven finally opened up and the sun shone its warm rays on my face. I stopped, closed my eyes to embrace all of the beauty of earth's elements surrounding me as I sat flat on my bum. The faint chatting of the small group of people, the gentle wind whispering, "You made it," the smell of fresh, crisp air, my heart smiling silently, and my soul ignited with spark. A deep voice lovingly and proudly said, "You made it!" My angel reached out his hand to help me up. Yes, I indeed did it! I didn't give up. I looked around and allowed myself to just be in the moment. This is life! To be in this 360-degree majestic wonder! I am in heaven on earth. That epiphany did hit me like Tammie had predicted.

At that moment, standing on top of the world, eye to eye with the Andes Mountains, my entire being knew no fear. I held out my arms as if mimicking Rose in *Titanic*, closed my eyes and welcomed in renewed strength, adventure, change, abundance, truth, freedom, and the rebirthed me—*the new divine humanness of my being.*

I have set sail on the journey of my new becoming, and I now fully trust God and the universe to be the captain of my ship. I know I will always be guided with His shining light to arrive at safe harbor. I simply need to trust and believe in myself, my unlimited potential, and all that this life offers. After all, I hold the belief in my heart that there are always greater and divine forces bigger than we could ever imagine. I just have to release control to that higher being and live! This knowing provides me with everlasting hope to move forward and upward and to "keep on keeping on"—a famous reminder from my Godmother Daylene and mom Saly.

"We have this hope as an anchor for the soul, firm and secure."
—Hebrews 6:19

My travels to Australia and Peru were God's winks that allowed me to clear all that no longer served me and reminded me to radiate my light, to share my gifts, to see simple beauty again, to allow self-truth, and to live simply. It took me away from the complexity of life's treacherous demands and society's (and my own) expectations. It took me back to rediscover my soul and to restructure the molecules of my being. It gathered all of my fears, worries, stress, depression, sense of lack, shame, embarrassment, and stagnancy...and blew it way out into the galaxy to dissolve into stardust.

God is my bank account. How can I ever worry?

As I complete this chapter for this beautiful book *Set Sail,* the wind carries the mainsail of the ship towards the completion of my next book, *Garden of Hope.* Four years ago, I set out on an unknown journey to discover the truth of my father and leave his compassionate and heroic legacy behind by sharing his essence through my story.

Now, as I glide on the unknown sea, with sometimes smooth and often-times challenging waves, I am creating my own legacy. I pour all my trust into the universe. I know for sure that the sun always shines above the clouds and I can always expect a beautiful sunset.

Life, I am ready to set sail on amazing adventures with you.

"Never be afraid to try something new. Remember, amateurs built the Ark...professionals built the Titanic."

—Author Unknown

AFTERWORD

I dedicate this essay to my auntie, Salorn Thou, who earned her wings and is now dancing in heaven with my father. She made it to her ninetieth birthday and left earth a couple of weeks after our time spent together. Nothing in life is coincidence. Life is temporarily loaned to us for a short time. We must embrace it, for every moment that we are alive is truly a blessing.

Special Gift

Receive and see more deeply into your TRUTH with a FREE 30-minute Life Coach and Energy Healing Session with Alis. Contact Alis at **gardenofhope11@gmail.com** to schedule your session.

Alis Mao is an energy healer, Life Coach, and founder of Wings of Love Healing group. She is a featured author in *Set Sail,* co-author of *Pioneering the Path to Prosperity,* a mother, lover of love, compassion, nature, and all of life's simple beauty, a giver, and a truth seeker. Her story is also featured in the book, *Sisterhood of the Mindful Goddess.*

Alis's upcoming memoir, *Garden of Hope: My Journey from the Killing Fields of Cambodia to a Life of Unconditional Love, Forgiveness, Compassion, and Trust* will be published by Flower of Life Press and released in 2020. Alis lives in Oregon with her two sons.

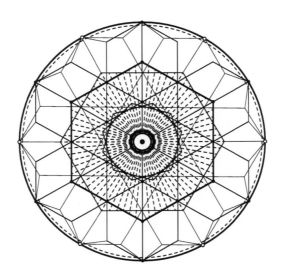

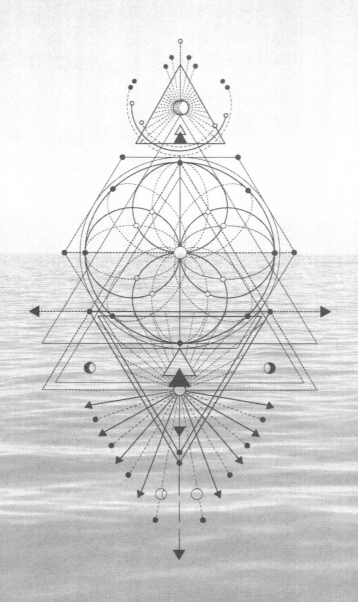

My Path as a Priestess: A story of Magic and Miracles

BY ARI HAFF

"Set Sail

Set Sail

One thing becomes another

In the realm of the Mother"

My story is one of surrender. Deep surrender and release, held in the loving embrace of the Great Mother. It is a story of dissolution and transmutation. It is a story of magic and miracles. It is a story of accepting myself and my calling. And it is a joyful reflection of how my path as a priestess has completely changed my life.

I have always considered myself a scientist. The practices used in science have always sung to the part of me that loves to explore this world, ask questions, and then find the answers. Facts, absolutes, and hypothesis proved or disproved either way, fulfilled my mind's need to *know*. It fueled my belief that in knowing I would be better equipped to steer my vessel through this life with fact-based control. Along with my facts, I added plans to my must-haves. And I mean *plans*. I had plans A through Z, and then for each of those I had backup plans. I funneled so much attention and energy into gaining knowledge and creating plans, and even *more* into implementation and attempts to maintain the surefire courses I set based on them. Yep. I was truly a capable and knowledgeable captain, and I took pride in this. Until it would all crumble.

Inevitably, some outrageous against-the-odds thing would happen and blow all my facts and plans out of the water. I would be left with a sinking ship and the remnants of soggy plans and supposedly supportive "facts" now exposed as the illusions they truly were. Yet, for years, I would continue this cycle, certain it was something I wasn't doing right. Somehow I messed it up. I must have miscalculated or was not committed enough, adept enough, or knowledgeable enough. I was too naive, too hopeful, too...*blah blah blah*. Over and over and over.

Along with my endless quest for knowledge and control over my life, I carried a deep feeling that I was missing something crucial and vital to who I am and why I am here, some piece that would make all the fractals cohere into something important, something that I didn't completely understand. I could feel it, even if I could not quite put my finger on what "it" was. And *ohhh*, I missed it. Yearned and longed for it even. It dwelled shapelessly ever-present deep in the back of my awareness, softly and persistently singing its call.

This mysterious calling started to get louder during a hugely transitional and challenging time in my life. The ways in which I had always done things, how I had not only survived but succeeded weren't working anymore. My life had shifted tremendously, and I felt scared, lost, and unsure of my future for myself and my family. During this time, my mother suggested that I read a book that she had found that resonated with her deeply. She felt that it included many of the thoughts and beliefs we had discussed over the years. Its subject matter was not anything I had read about before. Parts of the whole I had found in different philosophies, religions, and belief systems, but I had never seen so much of what I felt as truth together in one place, other than in my own mind before reading it.

The book was about a young woman finding her path and lineage as a Priestess in our modern world. It changed everything for me. It was all so familiar. It began to weave together so many of the threads that I carry. And it showed that there were most likely others like me out there, somewhere. That book launched me on a journey to find them, which became a journey to find Me.

While reading the book I began having dreams and memories that would surface so strongly they were impossible to ignore. I remembered life-times as a Priestess. Ancient lineages in distant and ancient lands. Living in community with my sisters in devotion to our Great Mother and in service to the people. I remembered rituals and ceremonies and places I had not known in this lifetime. Beloved faces and songs. I also recalled other dreams and knowings that I had experienced throughout my life that were similar and now made so much more sense. The memories and dreams were as real as my memories from my current life. These memories ignited a spark, and the calling became clear, loud, and undeniable.

I began to search for Priestesses. I needed to find them and to be with them and to learn all they had to teach and hopefully, to remember even more. I tried to find more about the author but found very little. I researched a place that was mentioned in the book that had brought back so many remembrances. I even looked for Priestesses in general, but what I found was not what I was looking for. It was frustrating and sad. So close, yet...

In time, I stopped actively looking but continued to hold the knowing within me. A few years later, I stumbled upon a face online that once again redirected my path. I don't remember what I was doing online that day, but I remember the feeling I got when I saw the ad. *Priestess.* My whole body reacted. I was excited, though still a bit reserved because of my findings up to that point. I followed the link and landed at a page about a commu-nity and mentor of modern-day Priestessing. As I scrolled through the page I came across a photograph of the mentor priestess. Everything else just stopped. I knew her!! Like *knew* her. She looked so familiar that my heart ached. However, as I sat there, I realized that I had never actually met this woman. I didn't know her. My reaction didn't make sense, so I did what I always did and started to research. I went to her website and then followed from there to the site of the mother lineage of which she was part of. The further in I went the more my heart sang. I even found other mentors like her who offered programs and circles. I considered all of them but couldn't shake the draw I had to the first Priestess I had found. So I returned to her site and read everything I could find there, and signed up for whatever offer-ing she had available, having no real idea how I had just changed my path once again.

Over the next five years, I threw myself into the initiate training in the 13 Moon Mystery School, guided and held by my dear sister and mentor Kalila through the Priestess Presence Temple. With each new step on this path I was remembering and rediscovering myself and my lineage gifts and skills that I carry. Also during this time, I continued to meet other sisters who I "knew"—not from this life, but I instantly recognized them on some deeper level. It was so joyful! It was like coming home to a home that you are only beginning to remember was so dear to you. Being with others who understood me and had similar remembrances, knowings, and skills was an incredible gift itself.

Divine Feminine Archetypal study is one of the foundations of the 13 Moon Mystery School and is derived from *The 13 Moon Oracle* by Ariel Spilsbury. This profound study led me through personal alchemical trans-formation unlike anything I had experienced before. As I deepened with each Divine Archetype and their light and shadow qualities, I learned to own those qualities in myself. I learned to embrace and develop that which serves and to work with personal alchemy to release or transmute that which doesn't. The changes that I have witnessed in my life, and in others' lives, brought by this work fills my heart with such joy and is consistent encour-agement to continue.

I don't want to mislead you. This path is a "road less traveled" for a rea-son. It is not an "easy" path. It is a path full of change, challenge, and radical self-responsibility. There have been times where I wondered if I really had what it would take to do the work on myself that I knew I needed to. I ques-tioned whether I could truly go the distance. That's a funny saying for this really, for this path is never ending. There is no finish line at completion. It is a spiral path that comes around again and again. So if you didn't clear or embrace it the first time, you will have another, and another, and another chance to do so. I have been astounded at the layers I have discovered so far, and I am sure there are still many more yet undiscovered.

In its quintessence, this path is one of love and service to Self and to the One. It is about changing our world for the better. It is not about changing anyone other than self. Through choosing to release anything that stands in the way of walking as love and focusing on embodying the parts of self that aid that walk, you become the change that is needed in the world. You not only affect your own life but those around you with the way you choose to be. When someone truly steps in as a Priestess in service, then they choose to share the skills and practices that they have learned in their own journey with others. It is not the work of a Priestess, in my lineage, to fix or change anyone else. My work is within myself and then in the offering to share what I have learned and to hold safe and sacred spaces for others who wish to also do this work for themselves. And then, if they are called, to support them to carry it forward to others as well. This is how this path shifts our world: shifting frequency, one individual at a time, thus raising the frequency of the whole.

One of the Divine Feminine Archetypes that we deepen with is the Great Mother. She embodies many nurturing traits, such as nourishment, holding, unconditional love, sanctuary, receptivity, and inclusion. This is often the first archetype a person new to this path deepens with because it is a beautiful introduction into the power of unconditional love, for yourself and others. Giving and receiving. One deepening practice into the Great Mother is to create a safe sacred space where you can empty out the mind, relax, and lean into her loving embrace, physically and spiritually. Let go. There is nothing to do. Just be. Be loved. There is no way to not be loved. It just is. The experience of this practice in itself is transformative.

The first time I allowed myself to truly let go and lay back into the Great Mother I had the most beautiful, nourishing, and mind-blowing experience. I set up soft pillows behind me, leaned back, and went into the state of empty presence. As I relaxed and allowed my body to be fully supported and cleared my mind, I found myself in the void. It was peaceful. I felt completely held, supported, and loved. After some time of just being and allowing, I felt joy flow through me as I saw the void light up with stars. It felt as if I was witnessing the birth of the universe. And then I began to create galaxies from the apparent nothingness. It felt flowing and effortless all while I was being fully held. It felt good. *So good.* It awakened my awareness that I am always loved and held. I do have support, whenever I choose to accept it. There is another way. That experience was the beginning of another huge shift in me.

I began to be more aware of how my normal behavior—all my research and planning and attempts at control, pushing through, and assuming I had to do it all myself—was the exact opposite of this practice. I allowed myself to really look at it. I began to question whether my normal behavior was really steering my ship or if it was just a game I had been playing with myself so that my overactive ego could feel soothed by my attempt. Do I really have to do it all myself? I compared the flowing feelings of allowance and support I felt when I relaxed and let go of my attempts at control, to the tense and at times desperate grip, and recognized the constrictive feeling that I usually experienced. Opening to this exploration was a good first step for me in what has been a very long process.

You see, I am a bit stubborn. I can recognize patterns in my behavior that may be helping or hindering me quite easily—it is one of my strong points—but even when I do claim the pattern, I rarely choose to change it right away. I have a process. I usually recognize it, then watch myself continue doing it for a while longer, calling myself out and noting when and how. It's like a game to me, really. I know I am doing it. After I have played with it a while I will eventually hit the point where I am just done with it and then I change. Right then. Done. Once in a while I will skip straight to the change, but usually not. I think it is a part of the scientist in me. My way of convincing myself that my hypothesis/recognition is indeed true. One of these days I may tire of that game...maybe.

After a while I also started to note the outcome of both ways of being, controlling versus flow; and over time, I began to see the pattern. That constriction that came with my attempts to control? Yeah well, the constriction was affecting the outcome. I couldn't help but to see that the more energy I put into trying to control the less I actually manifested what I wanted. When I would gently and loosely hold a vision, without trying to control every aspect of its creation, when I relaxed and flowed and allowed the support I had found in the Great Mother, beautiful things manifested out of what seemed like thin air. It has been a wild experiment!

Some of the most astonishing manifestations have been financial. This became especially obvious last year after I went on a pilgrimage to France to deepen into the Magdalene. During this trip, I went through a profound shift into a state of deep trust and surrender. I had received so many clear messages that I was fully supported and only needed to open to and allow the support. It finally got through and I made *surrender and flow* a chosen regular practice. Soon after the trip I went through several initiations concerning finances that normally would have sent me spinning. But this time I was different. I had changed. I didn't allow the fear to drive me back into constrictive behaviors. I let go and I trusted. Every bit of my intuition and body let me know it was the right choice. And time and time again, the universe showed it was indeed so. Several times in the span of a few months, some financial challenge would arise, and usually in short order the solution would show up soon after. It was amazing. Money would show up from places I never would have imagined. Over and over this happened. And not just with finances but in all areas of my life. It seemed to be that the less I tried to plan, control, or "figure it out" and instead used my heart knowing as my guide, the easier things became. Even my relationships flourished and became healthier and more fulfilling. *Trust, surrender, flow, and receive* became my way. It was during this time that I stepped into the project of this book you are reading right now, excited to share this newfound magic. Things were good, I was happy, and I stayed there for some time until life threw me a curve that brought me to my knees.

I had believed, with good reason, that I had transitioned through menopause. Although my husband and I had been open to having another child, we were both at the stage of acceptance that I was now past childbearing. It hadn't been an easy transition. It was filled with sorrow and mourning for each of us in our own ways. But we got through it and were finally at peace with it. So I am sure you can imagine my surprise when we found out we were pregnant. It felt like a miraculous gift. Another example of manifestation. Excited, we began to dream into all that it meant.

A couple of days after getting the confirmation, my doctor ordered a test to find out how far along I was. The results were devastating. The test indicated that I had lost the pregnancy. I was stunned. I was gutted. I was angry. I didn't, I couldn't understand what the point of it could possibly be. It had taken so much to come to terms with the loss of my fertility. Just when I felt I had found peace, this happens. I went spiraling down the rabbit hole. Sadness. Despair. Loss. Anger. Resentment. I was not in the flow. I was anything but in the flow. I wanted to fight and scream and cry, and then I wanted nothing. I fluctuated between falling apart and numbness. Screw the flow. I knew nothing. Nothing made sense anymore.

Sometimes though, during my numb times, I noticed that I would stand as my own witness. Like I was watching myself choose to let this take control of me the way it did. Choosing to detach from the flow, deny trust, grasp at finding answers. And as normal for me, I allowed it and watched. When I was standing as my own witness I was still aware of all I had learned about trust. That part of me noted the choices I was making. It also noted what else was happening at the same time. As if it was a carefully designed experiment, I watched as other aspects of my life started to fall out of the flow as well. Suddenly, more unexpected financial challenges, joined by a myriad of other unforeseeable issues, seemed to pop up out of nowhere. My witness self-watched and noted and even pointed it out to my slowly healing, pain-filled consciousness. The correlation was too obvious to deny. In true character, I continued like this, allowing things to apparently fall apart around me, aware of the layers and implications.

I did this until I was done. One day, I realized I didn't like the world I was creating, and although I was still sad, and I still did not understand the reason it had happened, I chose to let it go. I blessed it with all the love I knew I would have given the child and I released it. With that I then began to turn back to the flow, knowing and feeling the truth and wisdom of this path.

So once again, I am being delighted by watching my world shift in wondrous ways as I continue to surrender back into trust. Into the unknown. Back into the embrace of Great Mother.

I trust, I surrender, I flow, I receive.

Special Gift

GODDESS OF LOVE ARCHETYPAL DEEPENING PRACTICE—LOVE MYSELF BATH

This nurturing archetypal deepening practice is inspired by the Goddess of Love and encourages nourishment through our senses, and self-care. You will receive a beautiful PDF download with all of the steps and guidance on how to prepare and enjoy this practice, as well as a BONUS recipe for a luscious bath blend, and a recommended supplier list of where to find the best ingredients.

Access here: **www.thesapphiretemple.com/set-sail-book**

As Gatekeeper of The Sapphire Temple, **Ari Haff** is deeply committed to holding temple space for all ages and genders guided by the study of Divine Archetypes, the wisdom of the Sisterhood of the Rose, and the teachings of the 13 Moon Mystery School, derived from The 13 Moon Oracle by Ariel Spilsbury.

Through The Sapphire Temple, Ari offers monthly moon circles, guided divine archetypal study, as well as personal and group ceremonies. Ari also conducts varied events designed as sacred deepening experiences into essential oils, botanicals, sound, art, oracle, and embodiment practices.

Ari is a practicing Scent Priestess of the Emerald Temple. She is devoted to the sacred art of Anointing and to sharing the powerful gift of sacred oils. She continues her journey of remembrance as a Mentor and Temple Pillar in the Priestess Presence Temple where she found her path as a Priestess along with the beauty of true synergy and sisterhood.

As a Virtual World Creatrix and Artist, Ari builds beautiful realistic meeting spaces, temples, and sacred art in the virtual world. These spaces are designed to bridge the physical distance of global communities, spark remembrance, and offer a joyful reflection of the nature of our user created reality.

Ari is Mom to six wonderful children. She lives in rural Michigan with her family and their menagerie of cuddly cats, adorable goldendoodle puppies and one seemingly invincible goldfish.

Connect with Ari at **www.TheSapphireTemple.com**
Instagram: arihaff; thesapphiretemple
FB: Ari Haff @sapphirepriestess; The Sapphire Temple

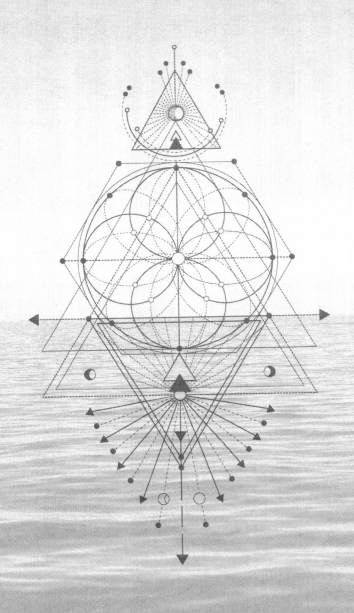

Giving Up the Good Fight: Learning to Trade Force for Flow

BY DR. RIMA BONARIO

She stood looking out the kitchen window, transfixed, proud, and maybe even a tiny bit jealous, as she watched her eight-year-old wisp of a daughter struggling to teach herself to ride a bike. All the girl had was an adult-sized bicycle making it incredibly difficult. Over and over she tilted the bike toward the ground, put her foot on the pedal, and tried to mount it. Over and over, she fell. Until, at last, she didn't.

I have no recollection of this story, but my mom tells me it was the moment when she knew beyond doubt that I would be okay in the world. I would find a way or forge a way if there was none yet. I may not remember it, but I know it. It feels like me. Getting over on that bike. Fighting my way onto it and making it bend to my wishes, fighting the good fight.

That trait, that persistence and sense of, "I can, and I will," served me well over the years as I stacked up significance and accomplishment. Until it didn't anymore, until it became a master that stole my freedom and my joy.

WHEN FIGHTING FAILS

I am on a deck at a rented cabin. It's slightly too hot in the full sun, but it feels so good to be sunbathing in the nude. I really want to move to the shady deck on the other side of the house, but I know I will be more visible there, so I endure the sun instead. *I can and I will.* The forest around me smells so good. I love feeling the cool breeze and listening to the birdsong. I focus on that as I try to ignore the burning sensation on my back. I catch myself enduring the heat and realize it's silly. My creative powers kick in and I think, "There's got to be an umbrella in the garage." I head to the garage and there it is. It's old and dusty, but no matter.

I feel pretty smart.

It's stuck behind some stuff, but that barely fazes me. As I wrench the nine-foot umbrella free it bangs me pretty hard on the toe and the rubber cap on the end comes off. Small setbacks. Nothing I can't overcome. I heave it onto my shoulder and start marching it out through the house toward the back deck, aching toe and all. I am smarter than this thing.

I get it out to the porch. I am so pleased with myself. But the umbrella won't open, and I can't quite figure out how to get it to do that. In my struggle to force it open I snap one of the wooden spindles.

What the fuck!

I am scandalized. Instantly I go from feeling smug and smart to feeling ashamed and idiotic. What was I thinking? I have spent the last three years focused on being a good receiver, learning to let go of my super-woman self who tries to force things to happen. My body is registering shame in every cell. I quickly return the umbrella back to the garage.

I pick up my towel and swimsuit and head over to the shady deck and lay down. The dappled sunlight dances over my body and the cool breeze and birdsong return. It's wonderful in that spot. Heavenly. I realize it won't be a problem at all to slip off my suit. As I lay there contemplating what has happened, I start laughing.

I have been doing this exact thing my whole life. I can see it all broken down with crystal clarity:

I am in a situation that isn't working for me.

I ignore that and endure it anyway. Until I can't anymore.

Next, I try to fix it. I get really clever. It soothes my ego as I find ways to twist and bend and outsmart the situation. I feel strong. Safe. Take that!

But it's lipstick on a pig.

I can see now that I had another choice. I could just step away from what I don't want, from what no longer works. I could look around and find what I *do* want and move toward that.

I get on Amazon and order a new umbrella, thankful for the lesson.

I don't think my story of learning to fight for what I have in the world is unusual. A lot of us were taught that you have to fight for everything you get in life. Most of the women entrepreneurs I know fall into this trap at one point or another. We are running our lives, our businesses, and even our families this way. Fighting the good fight. But what happens when the fight stops working, or when our battle-scarred bodies just can't go on that way anymore?

We can sense there is a better way, but we aren't quite sure how to get there.

FINDING FLOW

I am standing on the top deck of a small yet luxurious Dahabeya sailboat looking out on the dark blue waters of the Nile. I am in Egypt sailing peacefully down this luscious river, the Mother of Life. This is a dream come true and it feels like a miracle to be soaking in the Egyptian sun.

Several months earlier I felt a call from deep in my soul to travel to Egypt on a spiritual quest for my fiftieth birthday. I shared this with a group of girlfriends who were part of a monthly circle that we jokingly called a book club. The response was electric. We all felt the power of it zip around the circle. Everyone was excited and keen to go. I reached out to a friend who led tours of this kind, and we booked a date for the trip. Three of my friends signed up immediately. Three more were seriously considering it. I was feeling pretty great about filling the spots I had agreed to fill. Unfortunately, by the time the trip rolled around, things had changed. I was bringing just me and one other woman. I felt like a failure. Fortunately the trip went forward because my co-leader filled the slots.

But as I stood on the deck of that boat, every negative judgment I had toward myself was erased. I heard the Goddess whisper in my heart, "Welcome home." My heart swelled with so much love I thought it might explode. Then my insides melted into pure pleasure. I lost track of time and have no idea how long I stayed in this altered state of communion and connection. When it passed I knew something radical had shifted in me. This is just one of a dozen spectacular experiences I had in Egypt. We conducted rituals in ancient and powerful temples, including in Isis' temple in Philae and in the Great Pyramid. No words can ever do justice to the deep and lasting transformation that happened for me on that trip.

The Mother Nile herself was one of my greatest teachers. As we sailed her sacred waters for six days and nights I learned more about Flow than I could have ever expected. Before the trip was over, I heard the goddess's voice one more, "Bring my daughters home to me." She was asking me to return to Egypt the following year with a group of sisters. I made a vow to do exactly that.

STAYING IN FLOW IN A WORLD THAT VALUES FIGHT

I had heard for years from many teachers that I needed to trust the Flow rather than trying to push things through or "make it work."

But Egypt taught me that trust isn't enough. We are called to not only *trust* in Flow, but to *partner* with it. I understand that at a cellular level now. Flow is a state of being. It's a sense of being led and also of following. Sometimes the current is moving so swiftly you can just coast as it takes you with it. Other times the pace is lazy, and it may seem like you will never get there. Partnering with Flow means you develop the intuitive capacity to know when to put your oars in the water to slow or steer your vessel and when to paddle to move yourself forward.

After returning home, I booked the next trip myself and invited a colleague to teach with me. I was now committed to filling the entire trip. It was the highest priced offering I had ever created. I was scared. This was no small feat as I needed to fill the trip while simultaneously moving my family across the country. We had to prepare and sell our home, pack and ship our belongings, and find and move into a new home. We were between homes for seven weeks and I was working from Airbnb's and friends' basements. I doubted. I worried. I stressed. Until I remembered to partner with Flow.

I kept putting myself back on the deck of that boat, feeling the Nile river beneath me, remembering the Flow I felt there, remembering what my cells learned in Egypt. Every time I sent another chunk of money to my Egyptian tour company, I prayed for guidance, for my part in the process to put the word out so that those who were being called home would hear it. I surrendered my plans, my ego's desires, my list of who I thought should enroll and focused on being of service to the Goddess and the sisters who felt called to come home to Her.

Eventually, I came to see that partnering with Flow was also partnering with the Goddess Herself. Over the months, I came to feel Her presence in my life palpably as we partnered on this project. I didn't do it perfectly, yet She never withdrew from me. There were hiccups and delays. There were cancellations and fears that needed to be calmed. But in the end, I headed back to Egypt with ten women. A ten-fold increase from my first attempt!

GIFTS FROM THE GODDESS

I am at sitting in meditation under a field of golden stars on a deep blue background painted on a domed ceiling in my room in southern Egypt. I drop in deeply and whisper to the Goddess, "I have returned home. And the daughters you have called to you will arrive tomorrow." I feel Her presence surround me. Suddenly my inner eye opens, and I see Isis standing about fifty feet away from me at the altar in a colorful Egyptian temple. There are lighted torches on the columns that line the aisle on both sides. Isis motions for me to come toward Her. I have a moment of doubt and open my eyes. *Am I making this up?*, I wonder.

I close my eyes again and She's still there, beckoning me. I float down toward Her and She gestures upward urging me to go up. I float toward the top of the temple above Her. It is shaped like a pyramid. Across the apex is a stone tablet. It has a male name inscribed on it and I know that the name was placed there first by Moses and then replaced by Abraham. I don't fully understand, but I realize it's about passing on the linage and access to sacred wisdom. I know that I am being given the opportunity to erase that name and put a new male name in its place. But I have no son to pass it to. I think about putting my daughter Sophia's name there instead. But that feels wrong. It should be for all the children of the world.

I let out a wild roar from deep inside me, "It's for all the children! It's for all the children! It's for ALL the children!"

In a flash my body reels around until my back is to the apex of the pyramid. My legs stretch and open along the sides of the pyramid widening out as all of creation begins to tumble from my yoni. I feel the birth of the gasses and stars that make up the Universe, I feel galaxies and planets tumbling from within me. I birth our beloved Gaia. I feel all her plants and animals spilling wildly out of me. The diversity of life is breathtaking. I am utterly mesmerized by the beauty of it all. Then the people come, in a parade of human history, the dark and the light, the good and the bad; it's all there. And then I give birth to myself. My consciousness moves down into my body and the birthing continues as I give birth to my daughter Sophia. I am so overcome with love for her and in that instant I know how much the Goddess loves me, and all of creation. In that moment I understand that I am being shown the truth of who I am—a goddess who gives life. I see the fractal nature of the Goddess of All and the goddess Rima.

I had called the tour Awakening the Goddess Within. Well, She certainly did not disappoint. We went on to have the most extraordinary pilgrimage as we sought to awaken the Goddess within each woman who had made the voyage home to The Mother.

It was beyond anything I could have imagined or planned. This is the grace of Flow.

SAYING YES TO FLOW

Has your soul been inviting you to step forward in a bigger way? What is the big, bold, bodacious dream program that you are longing to create? What life goal or bucket list item is tugging away at your heart? What is your soul's legacy?

If you have been struggling with offering a high-end program for fear you won't fill it or that it won't be good enough, I urge you to listen deeply to your soul. If you have been delaying work on that book your soul keeps begging you to write for fear it won't be good enough, I urge you to trust fully in your guidance. Take a step. Just one step. Moving forward toward your dream is the only way it has any chance of coming to fruition. Whether you get there the first time or, like me, needed a couple of tries, the process of stepping out on faith will grow you in the most luscious and unexpected ways. And remember, you won't be doing it alone. Partner with the power of Universal Flow and watch the miracles unfold in your life.

In March of 2020 I will make my third pilgrimage to Egypt and it will be the most powerful yet. I can hardly wait to see what mysteries, magic, and miracles await me and my co-journeyers as we set sail once more on the sacred waters of The Mother Nile.

I continue to integrate these teachings into my life, to recognize my innate value and creative potential, to practice partnering with Flow in service to Life, and to love and be loved like the miracle I am. I don't know what else the future holds for me and my work in the world, but I believe that as long as I am willing to continue growing in my capacity to partner with Flow, keep showing up for Life's Lessons, and seeking to be of service, I will feel fulfilled and satisfied with the legacy that effort produces.

And you? Flow is right here, waiting patiently for you to join the journey and set sail toward your own dreams.

It's your time. It's your turn.

Dr. Rima Bonario is a dream weaver, soul coach, and wild heart healer. Her life's work is facilitating and teaching processes and practices that bring about a re-connection to our inherent, sacred wholeness.

Rima speaks and teaches on women's sovereignty and awakening. She offers in-person and online workshops, group and private coaching programs, as well as through hands-on healing sessions. She weaves together elements of modern science and ancient wisdom, myth and archetype, ritual and ceremony, and Soul/shadow work.

Rima's most recent offerings include body-based energy practices and explorations in the arenas of sexual sovereignty and embodied feminine presence.

Rima holds a doctorate in Transformational Psychology and has studied with Soul Mentor Sera Beak, Master Energy Teacher Lynda Caesara, Toaist Healing Master Mantak Chia, and Master Tantric Educators Tj Bartel and Charles Muir. She resides in Las Vegas, Nevada with her husband Tobias and her daughter Sophia. Learn more about Rima and her work at **rimabonario.com.**

Special Gift

MYSTERY, MAGIC, AND MIRACLES IN EGYPT

Join Dr. Rima Bonario as she takes you on a virtual pilgrimage and sacred tour of ancient Egypt. In this video gift to you, she will share many of the mysteries, magic, and miracles she experienced on her sacred pilgrimages. Dr. Rima will also share three potent practices that have allowed her to stop fighting the "good" fight and make the shift into a state of Flow.

Access here: **www.rimabonario.com/EgyptianFlow**

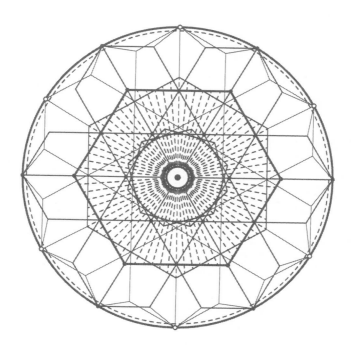

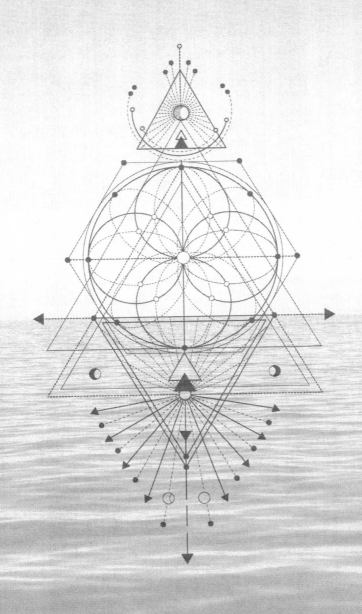

Holding My Own Hand

BY WINDY COOK

She caught me off guard when my soul said to me,
"Have we met?"
So surprised I was to hear her speak like that
I laughed.
The angel said, "Hold my hand and follow me,"
And so I did, into an ancient, dark forest.
"Now dig here," the angel said.
And so I did,
and I felt the strength
And an inner child begin to return.

—John of the Cross, Spanish Poet and Mystic, adapted from
"Dig Here, the Angel Said"

I'm setting sail, marking my coordinates for my destination and preparing for the journey onward.

Onward to my own legacy and the impressions that I will leave behind, long after I am gone.

The skies look mystical, promising. An azure mystery beckons me onward.

The wind is blowing from the south, the direction of curiosity, vitality, imagination, youthfulness, and innocence.

My destination is my legacy, "Winds of Change."

Yes, change is upon me both personally and upon us collectively.

Can you feel it?

I glance around the "ship" and there are six of us. *You and Your Inner Circle* is the name of the seminar and the perfect metaphor for my journey. This timely seminar is part of the *Growing Your Relationships* coursework of ThetaHealing™ workshops.

I am an author and a ThetaHealing™ Practitioner and Instructor.

It's all about energy.

It's all about consciousness, and ThetaHealing™ is as close as I've gotten to truth and real change.

> *"Although you appear in earthly form,*
> *your essence is pure consciousness."*
>
> —Rumi

ThetaHealing™ is a meditation technique that uses a spiritual philosophy for improvement and evolvement of mind, body, and spirit. Through this mediation process, one can connect to "Source," bring about healing, and change one's life.

"What is Source?" you may ask. Source is the *Energy of All that is*—the life force that permeates everything and everyone. It is the most intelligent, most loving energy in the universe. It is called by many names: Chi, The Great Spirit, God, Buddah, Goddess, Yaweh, Jesus, The Holy Spirit, Allah, Creator...

You and Your Inner Circle addresses the work you ultimately *want* to be doing and how to become more successful by surrounding yourself with the most positive influences. The work invites you to ask yourself important questions such as,

1. What is an inner circle of friends?
2. Who is in my inner circle of friends?
3. How do I know who should be in my inner circle?
4. Who will "batten down the hatches" if the seas become challenging and teamwork is needed?

My inner circle consists of my life partner, my children, and a select group of close friends and colleagues who have my back, inspire me to be my highest self, and those who I trust completely.

To live my legacy, I am called to connect to my highest self and to Source, trust my divine timing, manifest with abundance and clarity, and be aware of the company I keep.

You are essentially who you associate with.

It's a loaded statement, right? Loaded because so often we forget that we have a choice in the matter! Relationships can either drain or inspire us, but the dynamics can become cloudy and we find ourselves in the rescuer, victim, or hero connection. Blaming and pointing fingers or helping and healing another is characteristic of those familiar relationships. If the goal is to be our "highest" and best self, we should gravitate to those who resonate with that "sage" or wisest aspect of ourselves. That is not to say that we shouldn't be there for people who need us. But our inner circle should be people who bring us joy and happiness by their very presence. Have you ever noticed how you feel around certain people after spending a chunk of time with them? There is truth to the saying, "A person rubs off on you." Energetically speaking, that is exactly right.

We fill out the questionnaire and our instructor Dawna asks us which statement or belief we want to work on.

Dawna looks at me and asks me which belief I want to focus on.

"I want to work on, 'I have to be encouraged to succeed,'" I say.

Dawna walks over and sits across from me and begins to "dig."

Digging is a thoughtful set of questioning that allows a person to uncover underlying beliefs that reside in the subconscious that are obstacles to one's own growth, beliefs that have become outdated and no longer serve one's progress in life.

Muscle testing is key, because it accesses the subconscious mind for validation.

I close my eyes and take a deep, slow breath. I relax and go into the meditative or "theta" state of mind to access my subconscious.

In ThetaHealing™, the subconscious is where ninety percent of our thoughts and beliefs reside.

This is the place. The place where the "captain" of my ship is.

"Why do you need to be encouraged to succeed?" Dawna asks.

"I don't know," I say. "I need approval. I need to know that I'm doing the right thing."

"What is 'the right thing'?" she asks.

"The thing that isn't criticized or judged wrong by someone else."

"What happens if you are criticized?"

"I feel like I'm a failure."

"What happens if you are a failure?"

"I will be alone, lost, and I won't be loved."

"When did you feel lost and not loved?"

My eyes sink into the back of my head and I search backward in time. It's a dark passage back and I'm feeling blank. I suddenly become cold and scared, and I see.

"When I was five."

"What happened when you were five?"

I search again, and my eyes gaze upon the past.

"My mother went to law school and my father was not present."

"Can you tell me about that?"

I walk through the past now, searching for the feelings, the thoughts, and the answers as to why I need to be encouraged to succeed, why I need external approval to achieve my goals.

I was alone a lot. I was scared and uncertain. I felt so insignificant, unimportant, like I couldn't do anything. Like I was too small and clumsy. I felt lost.

"What did you need back then? What did you need when you were five that you didn't get?"

"I don't know."

"Ask her. Go back to that little girl and ask her what she needed back then."

I'm face to face with my inner child. She's so little, looking at me with big, wide eyes. She looks scared, frightened, and lost.

"What did you need, little one?" I ask her quietly.

There is a long pause and then she answers back, "I needed someone to hold my hand." She pauses. "I need someone to tell me it's going to be okay and that I'm not lost. That I'm strong enough to do anything."

The tears come and the pain rushes in.

Pain in my heart. Pain in my bones. I feel for a moment like I want to disappear.

The pain is unbearable, and it engulfs me.

I cry hot, painful tears, and they slide down my face like a faucet that's been left running for too long.

It's difficult to turn the faucet off.

Can I?

"Is there a belief about your life being scary and that you're lost, unimportant, and not strong enough?" Dawna asks.

"Yes."

"Do you want to clear that?"

"Yes."

The request is made to Creator and to the "Universal Life Force Energy," and then Dawna asks an important question: "What did you learn by being alone and not having someone hold your hand?"

I shake my head, not knowing what to say. How could I have learned anything from being alone and afraid and feeling unimportant?

I wait.

Then something comes into my mind. An answer.

"I learned about compassion. I learned how it feels to not have what I need. I learned what a person needs and how to encourage others."

"You learned something important about life or, in other words what we call a virtue, didn't you?"

"A virtue about others?"

I feel Dawna holding my hand.

She holds it for a long time. The past and the present merge and I sit there quietly. I feel a sense of peace, as if the little girl wasn't going to grow up until her hand was held.

She waited forty-two years to be acknowledged and have her hand held.

I push back the feeling of embarrassment because the feeling of healing my inner child takes precedence over two adult women holding hands.

My mind flashes to a quote by Vianna Stibal, the founder of ThetaHealing™.

"In order to develop, a child's brain needs encouragement, support, praise, a safe place to build their self-esteem, and to feel and learn love."

Encouragement. This is what my inner child is still seeking from others.

In looking back, my inner child didn't get encouragement. My mother wasn't a bad person; she was just too busy and, quite frankly, she didn't know how to nurture. She was the third of eleven children and was often alone and lost as a child. My mother raised me the only way she knew how. She raised a latch-key kid. I made my own breakfast, rode my bike to school, came home to a dark house, and made dinner.

Because my inner child didn't get what she needed, she was stuck. And I was stuck. All this time she was still looking for encouragement. She was still looking for someone to hold her hand. "I have to be encouraged to succeed" revealed itself as an obstacle that is holding me back from stepping into my power and my truth.

"You and Your Inner Circle" categorizes human development in three sequential categories of child, adult, and sage. As children, if we do not receive encouragement, support, and love, our bodies mature but our inner psyche remains a child. To move "forward" it is essential to revisit the "wounds" and forgive. Forgive our parent or parents who didn't give us what we needed, and forgive ourselves for feeling stuck, insecure, and not worthy. To forgive my mother, it helps to think about that parent as a wounded child too. My mother was essentially an adult child raising me. Being the third of eleven children, she had plenty of time with siblings but, like me, couldn't get enough of her mother. I have tremendous compassion for my mother when I think of her as a child.

Why is forgiveness important? Forgiveness is important because it takes up vital mental energy that can be spent productively moving forward.

Vianna Stibal talks about "The Three R's—Rejection, Resentment, and Regret" and how we need to clear them or our minds dwell on them, wasting an incredible amount of time. In essence, clearing the resentment I had as a child and forgiving my Mother was key in moving forward. I have freed up considerable mental capacity to move forward and manifest my "dream" job and move forward into my divine timing.

Does your inner child still need something? Have you ever asked her what she might still need in order to move forward?

If you listen you may find a treasure.

Then come the downloads, my favorite part of ThetaHealing™. These are new thoughts and beliefs from Source that create a new paradigm shift and affect real change.

"Would you like to know what it feels like to have compassion for others, and to know what support and understanding is without feeling scared and unimportant?"

"Yes," I respond.

"Would you like to know the Creator's perspective on what it feels like to be safe, surrounded by love and feeling a sense of importance? Would you like to know you were never really *alone* but being guided by Creator and 'the Energy of All That Is' to learn a virtue and that you were always loved unconditionally?"

"Yes," I reply, without hesitation.

With my eyes closed, I experience an energetic shift. It's difficult to put words to it. I also experience something else that feels really good.

I *marinate.*

That's Dawna Campbell's word for integrating new beliefs, healing old traumas, and experiencing Universal life Force Energy—and it feels juicy. Dawna Campbell is a Master of Science ThetaHealing™ Instructor, and I'm hosting her class.

It's really juicy.

Just like how a vegetable or piece of meat must feel when it's soaking up all that juiciness.

It's an amazing feeling, unlike anything I've ever experienced before. It's not intellectual. It's a feeling in my body. I also feel a shift, like a tree growing a new branch. My inner child has been able to finally grow up and, in turn, my adult self can experience an inner sage. This beautiful shift affects my inner circle, because instead of needing others to "encourage" me, others are now on equal ground and the power dynamic becomes more collaborative than parent-child. It's all connected. As we heal our inner child, major shifts take place, shifts that affect who we are to become.

It takes courage to get into that state of marinating. You have to be willing to uncover the uncomfortable feelings and painful emotions.

What is it going to take humanity as a whole, to have the courage to actually feel our pain and emotions in order to heal?

What is it going to take?

Do people need to know that there's light at the end of the tunnel and not just the pain that they will experience getting there? The seas can get stormy, turbulent, and dark.

Opiates and antidepressants are not serving us if they simply mask our pain and cover up our emotions.

Let us have the *courage* to feel it all.

I take a deep breath and look up at Dawna.

"Are you ready?" Dawna asks

I nod yes.

Once you realize that all comes from within,
that the world in which you live
is not projected onto you,
but by you,
Your fear
comes to an end.

—Sri Nisargadatta Maharaj

The ship is coming to shore, and I am at my destination. I walk upon the sand as a fully-grown woman on the inside and a Goddess on the outside, and I see walls of windows and the waves of divine timing rush over me.

Divine timing is when you are ready to walk into your soul's purpose and live your legacy.

It's a powerful time, and I can taste it. Many of us want to manifest a life's goal, but our divine timing dictates when that is.

The universe is unfolding in perfection and in ultimate grace.

I walk through the doorway of "Winds of Change"—an international center where ThetaHealing™ Instructors come from all over the world to teach and bring about change. This center is what I have been working on manifesting for years. I've written it down in specific detail, talked about it with others, and meditated on it. The only thing that's been holding me back is my own fear. Fear of failure. Fear that I can't do it myself unless I'm encouraged by others. I've walked through that doorway.

"Winds of Change" is here in Colorado with walls of windows to let the light and inspiration in, with classes such as *Basic, Advanced, Dig Deeper, Manifestation and Abundance, You and Creator, You and Your Inner Circle,* and *You and the Earth,* to name a few. We offer inspiring seminars that help people clear outdated beliefs so we can evolve, change, and grow. It's all about energy and consciousness.

"Winds of Change" is close to an airport, and instructors travel here to collaborate, learn, and network. It's a beautiful place with a circular meeting area outside and aspen trees with wind chimes swaying in the breeze.

Setting Sail beckons my calling to be a liaison for "Winds of Change." I host international healers and I bring people together, to teach collaboratively with other ThetaHealing™ Instructors and to orchestrate global change.

Change is upon us...as a global evolution to our highest selves, operating from our "sage" minds.

We are one.

"Winds of Change" is my legacy.

And...finally, I'm holding my own hand.

Windy Cook is the best-selling author of *The Sisterhood of The Mindful Goddess* and contributing author to *The New Feminine Evolutionary,* and *Sacred Body Wisdom.* She is also the author of Following Windy, an interactive blog for hopeful mothers struggling with fertility issues at "Moms Like Me." Windy is a graduate of the Journey of Young Women Mentoring Girls Certificate

Training and enjoys holding "Winds of Change" sacred circles for girls, mothers, and women of all ages. She also has formal training as a physio-neuro trainer, is certified in Reiki II, and is a ThetaHealing™ practitioner and instructor.

Windy's path includes work as a family therapist at Denver Children's Home for troubled youth and as a third-grade teacher in an inner-city public school for gifted and talented children. She holds a master's degree of Social Work from the University of Denver as well as a master's degree in Educational Psychology from the University of Colorado, Denver. She is Phi Beta Kappa from Colorado State University.

Passionate about philanthropic causes, Windy supports educational, environmental, and other nonprofit programs that promote the well-being of women and children. Windy can be found in a nearby yoga studio, hiking, playing with her children, picking sage, walking her dog, or riding her bike in open space. She lives in Colorado with her beloved husband, three children, and golden retriever. Learn more at **www.windycook.com.**

Special Gift

FREE 30-MIN THETAHEALING
INTRODUCTORY SESSION

Type the words "ThetaHealing Intro Session" into the subject line and I'll reach out to schedule your session!

Access here: **www.windycook.com/connect**

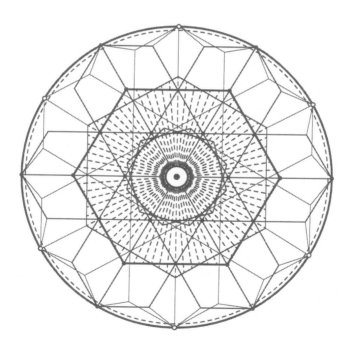

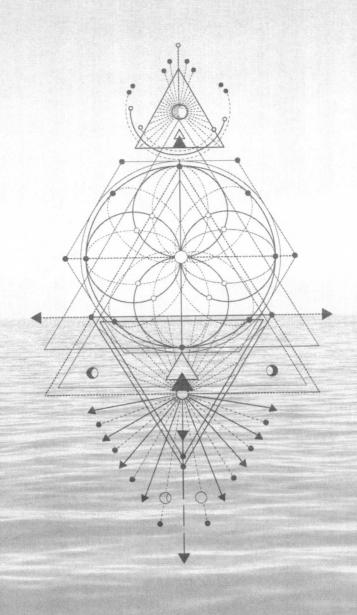

Journey to Self

BY ALISA ANTKOWIAK ADAMSON

We had recently moved to Oklahoma to settle. We had lived on both coasts, but for the first time in my life, I was called to move back to my husband's home. The wide, open spaces and land were calling me, and when I receive clear guidance from within, I don't hesitate. Unfortunately, it was not in the cards for us to move to our "land" right away. We had to go with plan B, which was to move into a small house in a bustling neighborhood. At one time I had fantasized about our family living in a yurt. What's funny is that our little house that I chose purely on the fact that it backed up to the "green space," was basically a more functional version of a yurt that our big family had the opportunity to simplify into. I really loved that little house, but the time started ticking and I began to get a strong itch for our land.

Most days after I picked up my son Luke from football practice, I would make a right turn down a road named Covell. This was not the way home! I would suddenly realize, "Where am I going?" and then right myself and drive the correct way home to our neighborhood. This happened so many times, that I realized it was a sign. One night, I said to my husband, "We are going to live down that road."

Between moving from California to Oklahoma, we lived with my parents on Cape Cod for a school year. It was time to leave California, and my Dad was sick. We had lived across the country from them for six years. It was time to reunite. My husband would stay to coach one more football season and until our house was sold. This was one of the most challenging times of my entire life. My parents had welcomed us with open arms. My Dad was so excited about it before we got there, preparing the house, getting bedrooms ready, and clearing space for us. It seemed to give him a purpose, according to my Mom. Then we arrived: myself, my four children, a dog and a cat.

My Dad engaged with us in the beginning, but quickly it became clear that he couldn't handle being around the kids for any length of time. He didn't feel well, he had very little patience, and he was on a lot of medication. So I spent my time flip-flopping between helping my parents and spending time with them and being a single parent to my children separately. It was an extremely stressful time. The silver lining was that I became closer to my Mom than I had ever been. We comforted each other, we shared with each other, and we supported one another.

It was also during this time that I discovered the online temple "Priestess Presence" and my spiritual life took a leap. I started meditating regularly again and participating in sister circles—really nurturing my feminine side. This temple was holding me up in a way I had never experienced before. I was mostly hiding it, though. God forbid I use the word "Priestess" with my Catholic parents! But eventually, I did. Eventually, I talked to them more and more about what I was doing, what I believed in, and what I aspired to. I can't deny that there were some angry moments and condemnation. It was while living there that it became clear that moving to Oklahoma was our next step. And so we did.

Ten months later, my father died. I was able to spend a full week with him shortly before he died, nurturing him with Reiki sessions and anointing him with Sacred Oils of Passage. It was one of the most beautiful weeks I had ever spent with him. He told me he wasn't going to die while I was there because I made him feel better. He had become much more open-minded in the end and entertained all of my mystical ideas and practices.

"I don't understand why you need a priest to come when you have a priestess sitting right here!" I joked.

"It's for balance!" he said, laughing. "I need both!"

He respected my spiritual path. That week, we watched documentaries on Mary Magdalene and the mysteries of Egypt. He loved the oils, and after I had to leave, my mother and sister continued the practice through his death. He told me that he would be with me, that he would meet me in Avalon, a spiritual pilgrimage I was going to take with the Priestess Presence temple that summer. He knew that we would be able to communicate after his death. I actually love our relationship now with all of the resistance gone.

A few months later, there was a cascade of events that told me we needed to start looking for our land now. On a whim, my husband pulled up some real estate on the computer. He started describing a farm with five acres, lots of outbuildings, fully fenced...and I asked him, "Where is it?" Sure enough it was down that road I always turned on. I immediately knew, this is it! So we made an appointment and went to see it. I loved it, and as I walked the land on that cold December day, my father was walking right alongside me, assuring me that we had found our farm.

I had always been a country girl, since growing up in western Pennsylvania, and I felt a longing to return to that. My husband and I, on our honeymoon twenty years earlier, had dreamed of the "petting zoo" that we would create with all the animals we wanted. Now, the dream of our own farm with our horses in the backyard was finally manifesting!

THE FARM

The farm expanded rapidly. Within days of moving in, our three horses arrived from my father-in-law's house. He was ready to be out of the horse business, and we were ready to be in! Within a week, we got chicks. We started with six and then three days later, we added three more. In the morning when we went to check on them, one appeared to be sleeping. I picked it up and it was breathing but didn't open its eyes. We carried it back to the house and I gave it some water from a dropper, but still the chick kept "sleeping."

I knew she was dying. I had to drive my kids to school, and my son Everet held her on the way there and I held her on the way home. I mixed some honey and apple cider vinegar in the water and gave her another dropperful. She drank it again, but just laid down on my chest for the next few hours until she took her last breath.

It was the first death on the farm. I wept for that little chick. Just a few weeks later we got two potbellied pigs and a month after that, two kittens. There were animals everywhere you looked, just the way we like it.

When my parents built our farm in Pennsylvania in 1987, I was intimately involved. I was a pleaser at that time in my life and I wanted to help—*and* make my Dad happy. I mostly took on masculine ways of being because this brought me more praise—fixing things, getting things done, working hard, achieving.

My father was complex and very emotional—something I always admired about him. Anything nostalgic—even church music—would make him cry. I know now just how sensitive and intuitive he was. But no one gave him the tools to deal with it. A young, white, Catholic male isn't taught how to handle "feeling" so much. My Dad carried pain, guilt, and sadness. His only tools were working hard and drinking. But back in his younger days, he was hopeful, he was energetic, he was fun, and he loved to play. Being in that energy felt good.

This is when I first met my horse Velvita, who stayed with me for the next thirty-two years. We grew up together. We had thirty-three acres and four horses, but not for very long. After only three years, we moved to Cape Cod. I thought I was going to live on that farm for the rest of my life. My favorite thing in the world to do was to ride my horse, in the woods, through a field, galloping away. This is what reminds me of who I really am. You know when you have that one thing that you do that feels so right, so invigorating, and fills you with life and possibilities? For me, this is riding. When we travelled back to Pennsylvania for my father's funeral, we went to visit the farm. It was the same. I toured my family around, and my son Grady said, "We need a farm like this." He was so right. Years later, I was finally going to have my sweet horse in my backyard again.

But no. I talked to Velvita about the farm we were buying, and she turned her head away. I assured her I would see her every day! I got nothing. I pictured living on our new farm, but I could never see her there.

She wasn't coming.

The next phase of my life would not include her. I must now learn to be without her, when I could have finally seen her every day. We drove to

Florida for spring break and she suddenly died while we were gone, just one week before our move to the farm. All this time I felt like I was keeping her going, whenever I would see her and still gallop through the woods with her. The truth was, she kept going for me. It was time for her to let go, and she didn't want me to stop her.

I have had the realization several times in my life when I hadn't ridden in a while, that when I did again, *I remembered me.* I was full of life again. I was connected again. My horse gave me this gift. There was a hole and so much sadness for me to look out at the three horses grazing without Velvita. My five-year-old daughter Lenora stood with me one day, looking out into pasture and said to me, "There she is, mommy! She's right there, with the other horses. She did come!" And it was true. I could absolutely feel her there. She is like a guardian angel. But I didn't have a horse to ride. We had my son's horse, Gracie, a semi-trained pony named Bo, and a sweet older mare named Tracy. But in just that synchronistic way that everything seems to happen, six months earlier I had met a horse named Phantom, a tall, blue-eyed, half-thoroughbred.

At the time, Everet was taking lessons at a stable and one day when we arrived, Phantom was there, all tacked up. The trainer said to me, "You know, Velvita isn't going to live forever, and Phantom is the perfect horse for you. Why don't you take him for a ride?" I refused to acknowledge Velvita's mortality, but I didn't refuse a ride with Phantom. He was very sweet and gentle. Everet was desperate for me to get Phantom. On Mother's Day, he wrote me the sweetest note and said he wanted to give me Phantom. My heart ached to have my own horse. So I finally did it. I had just attended a Rosa Mystica retreat, focused on self-love, so I knew I had to get him. I remembered again just how important riding is for me. As soon as I got home, I made the call. Now we have four! And the farm feels complete.

I attended two spiritual retreats, two summers in a row, with the Priestess Presence Temple. The core teaching of this Magdalena training is to walk as love. My practice is to fully embody this in my daily life. At the moment, our farm is healing our family. Each one of us—including the pigs, the chickens, the horses, the kittens and the land itself—enriches the other so very much.

My brother-in-law came to visit and said, "It's kind of like a rag-to-riches story for all your animals"...and it's true! We are *all* living the high life together. Everyone I know is drawn here. Recently a friend from out of town was passing through and asked if she could bring her daughter Elle and come visit. Elle's favorite thing in life was horses and she desperately wanted to ride. She had been in an accident and had broken her leg falling off a horse just a few months before. She had ridden since but had been uncomfortable. Our sweet and gentle horse "Tracy" would be the perfect fit.

The night they arrived, we hopped on our horses bareback: Everet on Gracie, me on Phantom, and Elle on Tracy. We rode around our property nice and easy, even walking through the pond to refresh. Elle didn't want to get off. She told me this was the first time since her accident that she felt like she used to—relaxed and joyful.

Now, our farm is complete. It's more than a petting zoo, it is a *healing farm*. I can feel my ancestors guiding me. I'm standing here poised to begin helping others outside of my family. Friends are telling me they can they can sense the farm's healing nature. My intention is to embody the fullest expression of who I really am. My truest, most pure self. Let go of all the rest of it. Awake, authentic, and full of love.

It's funny how life is cyclical. In so many ways I feel I have returned home to myself, my young self. And yet I have had so many experiences in the middle to take me to this place.

My close friend from college recently visited me on the farm with two of her children, commenting, "What you're doing and creating here is so you!" The Lisie she knew, the girl I was in college, would be living on a farm, using Reiki, and working with animals. This is the essence of who I am. No matter how many times I have thought I had "lost myself," I have always found "her" again.

Even as I struggled with illness, weight gain, and loss of energy these last few years, I received wise counsel from my teacher, Diana Dubrow. She made the sacred oils I used to anoint my father, and then I met her in person at the Avalon pilgrimage. Diana told me that what was happening with my health was because I had "forgotten who I really am." The young, energetic, intuitive, horse-riding girl who loved nature had gotten lost somewhere in the mix.

And now, here I stand, vowing to become the fullest expression of who I really am. The truth and the power of it. To be a beacon of light. To be a balance of the masculine and feminine. A mother, a mystic, a wild woman. A healer. A farmer. On my horse, galloping through the fields.

I call on my angels, guides, and ancestors every day. They all want us to succeed. This includes my Dad, Velvita, even the little chick, our past dogs, my grandmothers, and my highest Self. When I say *succeed,* I mean to be the fullest expression of who we really are, to find ourselves, and to walk as love. They are guiding us all the time. All you have to do is pay attention and listen.

You are not alone.

Sister, shine brightly so that others can see your light—it inspires them and gives them permission to shine their *own* light.

The light is on at the farm.

We are waiting.

Alisa Antkowiak Adamson (Lisie) began her journey studying Psychology at Dartmouth College while throwing the discus and hammer on the side. There she met her football playing husband, Chris, who continued on to devote his career to the sport. She worked with families in mental health and went on to get a master's in social work in hopes of making a bigger impact in the world. She coun-  seled students in boarding schools where she and her husband lived in New Hampshire and Connecticut until she gave birth to her first child. Lisie then devoted her life to mothering, long-term breastfeeding, co-sleeping, and three more pregnancies and home births over the next fourteen years. Lisie and her family moved to California and she spent those years at home studying nutrition, health and wellness, yoga, and spirituality. Lisie has studied horse therapy and energetic healing. She is certified in Space Clearing and Reiki. She has been married for twenty years and is the mother of Luke, 15, Grady, 12, Everet, 9, and Lenora Breeze, 5. Oklahoma is their home now—they live on a farm with dogs, cats, chickens, pigs, and horses.

Lisie is a truth-seeker and has always strayed from the mainstream. She is a lover of natural products, fresh juice, whole food, natural remedies, crystals, and essential oils. She loves nature and sunlight. She follows the moon and has studied the blood mysteries. She is now in her third year as a Priestess Initiate in the 13 Moon Mystery School lineage, where she has found meaning, magic, and sisterhood.

Lisie is expanding her gifts outside her family and into the world. Magic, mysteries, and connection to the earth and spirit is what inspires Lisie on a daily basis. She seeks to WALK AS LOVE as a way of life. Learn more at **www.Lisieatthefarm.com.**

Special Gift

HEALING WITH THE ANIMALS—MEDITATION

Do you want to learn to connect more deeply with the animals around you? Would you like to understand what they are trying to tell you and receive their guidance? With this meditation, you will deepen into greater connection so that you can receive their wisdom and love and heal into your wholeness.

Access here: **www.lisieatthefarm.com/setsail**

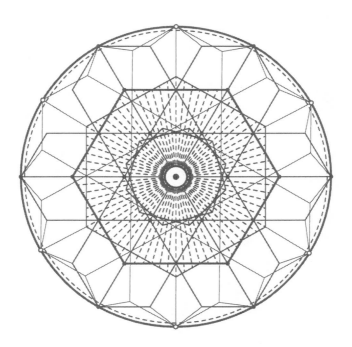

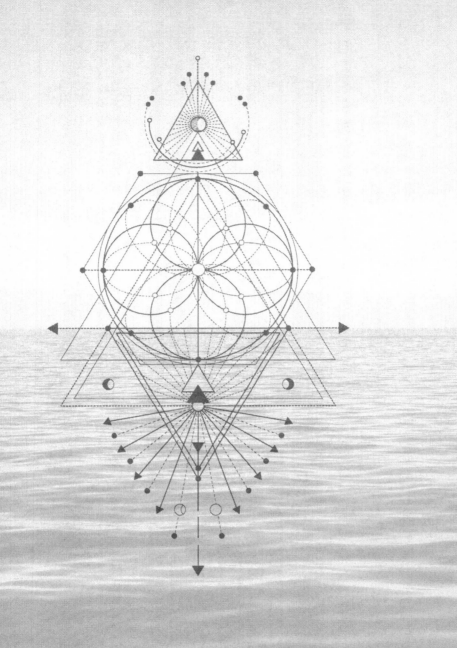

A Sacred Awakening: Breaking Free from Illusion and Surrendering to Love, Liberation, and Divine Union

BY DANIELLE ASHÉ

There once was a brave soul who accepted a sacred mission to visit a far-away place in another dimension called Gaia, the place that human beings referred to as planet Earth. This place had been in darkness for a long time and was in need of guidance. This brave soul's acceptance of this mission meant that upon arrival to the third dimensional physical realm, shifting from a state of pure consciousness into physical form, it would forget the Truth, the essence of oneness.

To fulfill her unique mission, she had to enter the third dimension on a specific date, in a specific city, in a specific country, into a particular family, into a specific physical body.

The people on Earth that shared her same gender and skin color were treated differently, as less than others, and because of this they suffered.

It was time for this to change, but the illusion of separation still lingered in the collective psyche.

This brave soul is me and this is my soul's story.

I chose to be born into a family among the first generation to move out of the city and out of poverty to advance economically, seeking better opportunities. My family provided so much for me and I never went without anything. I was very bright and creative and always tested far above average in the standardized tests. I was privileged in many ways, although I was still treated differently because of my gender and skin color.

My mother and father separated when I was nine years old and from that point in time my father was rarely ever around.

I did fairly well in school although it always felt rather boring.

I went to college because I felt pressured and it was expected of me, especially because people with my skin color weren't permitted to obtain degrees until fairly recently in our history. Deep down I felt like continuing on with more schooling wasn't something I wanted to do; I wanted the freedom to learn and explore life on my own terms, but was told that I was "too smart not to get a degree" and that "I needed it be secure, respected and successful in life," especially as a woman with my skin color, so I stuck with it.

I decided to earn a degree in Public Policy because I saw the injustices in the world and wanted to make things right; but early on in my studies, I realized that the change I envisioned could not be made through the government so I went on to earn a Master's degree in Educational Psychology and Youth Development while I worked full-time at the university to pay for my student loans.

I quickly grew tired of sitting behind a desk day after day staring out the window, wondering if there was more to life. I wanted the freedom to live my life, to do what excites me, instead of spending forty hours a week doing something that was of no real interest or importance to me other than the fact that it paid the bills.

It was confusing; I had done all of the things that one was supposed to do to achieve security and success, but I wasn't happy.

I had spent so much time sacrificing my dreams, passions, and deepest desires for safety that I felt my soul had slowly been dying.

I had a good job and a nice apartment, but yet I felt stuck and empty. I was unfulfilled and questioning the deeper meaning of life.

Every day I sat at the computer scouring the internet for the answers to all of my questions, wondering: What am I here to do? What's next? What's my life purpose? I didn't find the answers to these questions from my desk because "figuring out" my soul's purpose from behind a desk wasn't possible; I had to go out into the world to discover it.

I had completed my Master's degree and was in the midst of my first yoga teacher training, when it hit me loud and clear; as I lay there on my mat in savasana, my inner voice told me to save some money, sublet my apartment, quit my job, and go spend some time immersed in nature teaching yoga in Costa Rica.

Just a few months prior, I had visited the Afro-Caribbean Coast of Costa Rica for a women's retreat; I was transported back to that place, remembering how relaxed and turned on I felt and the sense of peace I felt while immersed in the rich abundance of Mother Nature, surrounded by exotic fruits and medicinal and edible plants growing wild. I also recalled how inspired I had felt by all of the people that I met who had left Babylon behind and created opportunities to make this their reality.

Plus, I had always loved the Spanish language and wanted to become fluent to be able to teach it to my children someday, and I wasn't getting any younger.

All I knew was that this sense of freedom I felt in Costa Rica was what I had been longing for. A 7-day visit wasn't enough; my soul yearned for more. This was the medicine that my soul was desiring. Costa Rica was calling me back.

Deep down I knew that if I just had the opportunity to remove myself from the day to day hustle and immerse myself in nature, the answers would be made clear.

Up until this point in my life, earning degrees and choosing a clear career path had been such a priority, so taking this leap of faith into the unknown felt scary, irresponsible and impractical.

I thought, "I must be crazy to leave all of this behind," while at the same time, I had always known that what I was meant to be doing didn't yet exist, that I wasn't destined for some titled, salaried position with an application and clear job description; I knew that part of my purpose was to create something new. I knew that the solutions to many of the world's greatest challenges had yet to be discovered and it was part of my purpose to bring them forth.

Until then I had been playing it safe, waiting for a secure opportunity to come along, for the logical next step for my future to appear, until the day came where I couldn't wait around anymore; playing it safe was no longer an option and I had to make a move.

The point came when the pain to remain the same became greater than the fear of the unknown.

The pain finally pushed me to the point where I had no choice but to leap; I had to make a move in the direction of what I desired and figure out what was next from wherever I landed. I finally found the faith that there was something greater out there in store, even though I had no idea what it was. I found the faith to fully trust that this longing within me would guide me in the right direction, and I had finally gained enough courage to take the leap and trust that the net would appear, and it did.

Making my way in the world once I had landed was only the beginning of a greater journey; little did I know that this was the beginning of a sacred initiation of deep remembrance.

At first life in paradise was pure magic, but as money began to run out, fear and insecurity crept back in. Again I became consumed with questions such as, "Who am I?" "What is my purpose?" With the added pressure of, "How am I going to sustain my life outside of the United States?" The last thing I wanted to do was go back to the hustle in the United States. "Was this lifestyle sustainable?" "Was all of this too good to be true?" I became so preoccupied with my survival and creating a source of income that was in integrity with my soul that it stole me from the present moment and became my priority in life; I became so focused on this that I forgot to enjoy what was right in front of me.

Yes I had left the United States and was living the dream, the "Pura Vida" or "Pure Life" as they say in Costa Rica, but after years of operating from a wounded feminine mentality, coming from the culture of lack, scarcity, and competition that's so prevalent in western society, I had yet to fully break free from this way of being; I was still carrying many of the fear-based programs and beliefs that were embedded in my subconscious mind. In Costa Rica, I could no longer hide behind a false identity and the sense of worthiness and security that my degrees and a fancy job title once brought me, because they no longer mattered.

Even though I had found paradise, I wasn't fully enjoying it. At times I felt completely lost and was filled with fear and anxiety about my future. I had been in survival mode, spending so much energy trying to "be in control" and "figure it all out" that I didn't allow myself to be fully present and in gratitude for what I had, where I was and how far I'd come.

My fear of the future and search for financial security became a catalyst; if this lifestyle was to continue to be my reality, I would have to overcome my fears, break free from my subconscious beliefs and create new ones that aligned with my desired reality. It was ultimately up to me to completely shift my relationship with fear, lack, scarcity and money.

These questions remained even as I found myself living a life that was beyond anything I could have ever imagined; living in a charming little nest made of bamboo in the jungle on a magical, sustainable permaculture food forest owned by a beautiful family, walking this path beside my beloved.

Living in the jungle naturally deepened my connection with Great Spirit, Father Sky, Mother Nature and I began to remember the ways of my indigenous ancestors while working with sacred plant medicines.

I discovered that living simply is sacred; the simplest things became sacred ritual while living so closely to nature.

The more time I spent in nature, the more deeply I de-programmed. I experienced a deep mental, physical and spiritual detoxification; the more I cleansed my mind, soul and body, the more clearly I could see the ways that human disconnection from nature and the illusion of separation has kept people from living in harmony within themselves, with the earth and with each other.

It seemed to me as if most people were living life completely backwards, that they were doing so much to *get* things that they thought would bring them what they desired, but all of this was actually taking them further from the deeper feeling they were seeking; many had sold their souls and had grown disconnected from their true nature, which lead to a greater sense of division, less connection, a more competitive nature, which made it so much easier for the powers that be to divide and conquer.

I witnessed the simpler lives of Costa Ricans and they seemed to be happier and healthier than people who seemed to have so much more based on first world standards.

Living in such abundance with a small amount of money was liberating; it opened my eyes and heart to the reality that money really doesn't make you happy, although it can be used as a helpful tool.

The natural environment also provided the spaciousness and awareness to get out of my head and become more present in my body. After years of living in fight or flight mode, the sounds and rhythms of nature began to heal my nervous system as deeper fears, programs and traumas began to surface.

I found myself moving through the depths of a dark night of the soul, questioning the nature of existence and praying for answers. In the midst of this, during the darkest time of my life, I received a message from my ancestors speaking loud and clear, " We see you, we are celebrating you, we are rejoicing; you have finally broken free and you have come so far, for all of us." Hearing the voices of my ancestors shifted something deep within me and everything began to make sense. All of the pieces of the puzzle started to fit together, and I could finally see the bigger picture.

From out of the furthest depths of darkness emerged a brighter light than ever before.

From this point forward, I've felt the guidance and presence of my ancestors. I felt supported and protected knowing that they had led me here, to live a legacy of liberation for my lineage; to break free from generations of suffering and oppression to heal the past, present and future.

The ancestors that had been stolen from Africa, taken to the United States and enslaved for generations were now celebrating my sacred liberation, which was also their own.

Much of my healing came in remembering and reclaiming my identity and sovereignty by connecting to my true nature, to the consciousness of my ancestors before they were taken from their native land and enslaved. Liberating my lineage from all of the pain, suffering, anger and fear that has kept us separate from our pure essence, which is peace, love, prosperity, expansion and unity, oneness with each other and the All.

It also came in my awakening; gaining the awareness that most of our judgment, assumptions and projections have only perpetuated further division and weakened our individual and collective co-creative power. A Course in Miracles explains that everything is either one of two things, an expression of love or a cry for love and we are here to discover a deeper sense of connection and compassion for all beings as Divine reflections of God.

This is the path of the Mystic; coming into deeper faith, trust and surrender into oneness and Divine union with all that is, was, and all that ever will be, in deep devotion to living as love embodied.

I began to remember that this was why my soul accepted the mission to come here to the physical, third dimensional plane, to planet Earth into this body; along with the realization that I needed to experience everything that had led me to this moment in order to fulfill my soul's sacred mission.

I've helped to pave the way for others by blazing my own trail; I needed to burn away everything inside of me that was not pure love in the alchemical fire, stripping away all illusions and all that was not real, and in this process I learned to fully trust and surrender in sacred union with the higher power.

I was now awakening to the truth and able to more clearly see my soul's purpose as a part of the sacred rEVOLution, a new way of seeing and being; a movement of humans co-creating as divine expressions of God, walking in the way of the courageous heart, letting love lead the way.

Fostering kinship and solidarity with those who are also carrying this deep love and vision for humanity, those who are here to shift the collective consciousness by courageously choosing to follow their hearts. Those who are ready to break free from the illusion of separation to live in love, liberation and Divine co-creation.

Because we *are* the change, we are the future and we're strong on our own, but far stronger, together.

I can now see that this journey has been about so much more than my relationship with money and security. (Although this has been a big part of this initiation and something that I will continue to explore.)

This journey has been about returning to nature to remember our true nature, *the* true nature; it's mostly been about finding the courage and awareness to allow my heart to continue to lead the way to remembrance, which is what my soul came here on Earth to experience.

Sometimes we must forget in order to remember who and what we really are—*Love*.

And once this is remembered, we mustn't let anything or anyone keep us from living in love and liberation, to truly *be* the love that we want to see in the world.

This is my return to Divine Love.

A Sacred Awakening.

And this is only the beginning.

DaniElle Ashé has been contemplating the connection between the human condition and spirituality since as far back as she can remember. A big part of her Soul's purpose is to raise collective consciousness through Sacred Activism, a practice that combines aspects of social justice, psychology and spirituality.

DaniElle draws from her interdisciplinary education and professional background as well as her personal experience with mysticism and various cross-cultural spiritual practices to assist others to come into alignment mentally, physically and spiritually and take inspired action lead from the heart to truly be the change they wish to see in the world.

Her message is one of universal love and union with each other and the divine. She believes that the cultivation of one's personal relationship to Divinity serves as a necessary bridge between the dichotomy of diversity and unity, which exists simultaneously, and that this sense of awareness is key to the evolution of human consciousness, because the real rEVOLution begins within.

She also loves to travel. Experiencing different cultures and witnessing the human condition across the globe has continued to broaden her personal sense of healing, growth, awareness, connection, and expansion. She's been breaking free from the illusion of separation by living a legacy of love and liberation not only for herself but also for her lineage and all of her relations.

When not traveling, DaniElle spends most of her time surrounded by nature on a sustainable permaculture project in the jungle on the Caribbean Coast of Costa Rica where she lives simply and works with sacred plant medicines.

Danielle is deeply connected to her indigenous roots; she's happily and humbly devoted in service to Mother Nature, Great Spirit, and her ancestors as she considers them to be her greatest guides, healers, and teachers.

Special Gift

CENTER THE HEART WORKSHEET

Ready to let go and fully allow your heart to lead the way to love, liberation, and divine union?

This reflective writing activity will activate and align you to your heart's deepest desires, revealing what your heart most wants to bring to the forefront of your awareness and your actions at this time.

Access here: **https://forms.gle/aJ4oj5DCP588pxzF9**

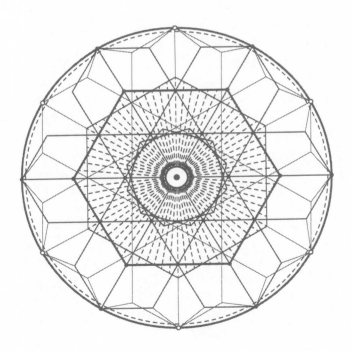

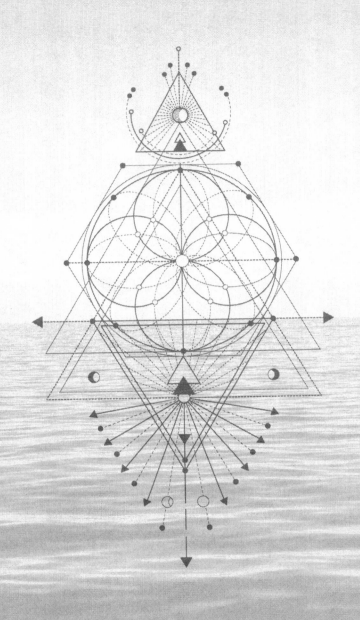

The Illumination of Your Divine Self

BY JAMIE BRANDENBURG

My parents did what most concerned parents would do. They took me to see doctors and therapists. "Can't you give her something? She's so emotional all the time. We're so worried about her."

Yes, I was emotional, and I had no idea why. What I did know was that my emotions did not feel normal to my family and friends. I felt like a misfit. When the doctors gave me pills to calm me, my wild child kicked and screamed. Who were these so-called experts who were poisoning me? I felt as if they were folding my long limbs neatly into a cube so that I would fit in a super-small box. And I've never been a fan of boxes.

I can tell you now what I couldn't then tell my younger, misfit self. "You sense more than most people, Jamie. Emotions wash over you like rainwater, and you need to find tools to help you so you don't drown, and also, so you can own the tremendous gifts you've been given to feel so intensely. You need tools to allow you to process all that moves through you so that you can be free to choose how you respond to the emotions you feel."

Instead, I spent decades feeling confused and lost, demanding that the universe show me signs, or I would take myself out. I couldn't see beyond my personality because I was so busy *acting out* my personality. I had unhealthy addictions, looked for love in all the wrong places, and had occasional suicidal thoughts.

I was slowly succumbing to the crazy that was my life when I was called to begin my personal illumination journey: A call to go to—get this—Idaho. Nothing exciting happens in Idaho, right? During a weekend retreat with a girlfriend, I met someone who had the energy tools I so desperately needed. He was from South America, and he didn't speak any English, but I could feel his calm and his connection to an inner wisdom. I knew he had things to teach me, tools that would save me from my current despair and overwhelming loneliness. I answered that call, and it started my feet on a journey of discovery that covered quite a few continents (I needed a lot of tools). I would like to share some of those tools with you.

How can we reconnect with our divine essence—our source of joy, light, power, and wisdom? How do we peel away the layers of defenses and labels that we've taken on and learn to trust our inner wisdom to guide us to live a radiant, rich, and reverent life, an illuminated life?

You're in the right place if you've ever felt that you're trying to be someone you're not, or that your life, no matter how perfect (or less-than-perfect) it appears on the surface, is not embodying the fullness of your essence, or that you're intentionally messing things up, hurting yourself and others so as not to have to be responsible for figuring out your true path.

When you truly desire to shift your reality, the right tools, people, and places find you as you open to receiving and applying new practices. Even if you feel broken, disheartened, and like you've tried everything before, you start with a simple desire to loosen your grip on your defenses and allow the possibility that something else might enter. When you open to it, this something feels expansive and freeing, compassionate and aware, patient and wise, strong and powerful. And this moment gifts you the possibility of expanding your awareness to experience a spark of your essence.

Here are some of the benefits of taking a chance on your luminary expansion:

- When you allow awareness to expand, you become less caught up in whatever has magnetized your attention until now: That relationship. That job. That addiction. That schedule. That family. That defeating self-image...
- Your expanded awareness allows you to bring more of yourself face to face with your current challenges or obstacles.

- You surprise yourself with fresh solutions and previously unnoticed resources.
- You no longer fear that life will pass you by without you blooming into the best version of yourself.
- When fear comes up, you're able to transmute that fear into support for your journey.
- You begin to cultivate a new strength and the ability to trust yourself again, even if just a little to start with.
- You live a life that inspires others to free themselves from their own stupor.
- You no longer feel small, reactive, angry, sad, confused, paralyzed, or limited.
- You feel juicy and alive with passion and integrity, able to find serenity no matter what is going on in your life.

Before we start, remember: It's your birthright to be wise and noble, loving and generous, and to treat yourself and others with reverence and esteem. It's your natural state to be constantly creating and renewing yourself, to be fully engaged in the world, and to bring your *all* to every moment of your experience.

Are you ready to dip a toe in?

IT'S OKAY IF YOU DON'T KNOW WHERE TO START

"Self-care has to mean more than a mani-pedi," sighed Julie. "I mean, I've taken a lot of self-development courses and it seems that there's a lot more to self-love than that. I want to know for sure what I really want, to go much deeper, you know?"

She smiled with a slightly worried look in her big sparkling brown eyes.

"I'm considering some really big changes in my life and I want to make sure I make the right decisions for the right reasons. On the outside, I seem to have it all together. I'm a top consultant in my industry, I lead people in the professional world all the time, and I love it. I travel the world offering strategic ways to enhance performance and sales. I guide corporations on how to implement organizational tools to enhance their leadership skills. I'm fortunate to reach so many people, and I'm so often rewarded with the success stories my clients share. My income is great, and I feel that I really make a positive difference in people's lives. My marriage is heaven-sent, and my son is adorable. On the outside, it seems I have the perfect life, yet there's something more. I can feel it."

Her brown hair cascaded down her shoulders as the light filtering through the window caught waves of auburn highlights. Her eyes glazed with a sadness she was trying to hold back, and her voice choked a little as she took a deep breath and gave it a shot: "There's a part of me that feels empty, you know? It doesn't even make sense! It appears I have it all...and yet, I don't. I don't even feel like I have the *right* to want more. Shouldn't I just be happy with what I have?"

As I listened through her words, I knew that she was not sure where to start. She could sense the inner undercurrents that were flowing and mixing together, yet she simply felt blocked. The truth was, it didn't matter where she started. It's all connected, so any start would lead us where we needed to go.

"I don't want to look for happiness on the outside, grasping for a less-than-fulfilling dream because I don't really know what I want...or do I? Will I ever be satisfied? Or will I just always want more? A mani-pedi can only go so far..."

She smiled and we both chuckled. It helped relieve some of the pain she was feeling.

"I just keep having ideas of adopting children. It's always been a dream of mine. My husband is in, no matter what I decide. We're a good team and he fully supports me. He just wants me to be sure. I do, too. Raising kids is a really big deal and a huge responsibility! I don't know if I really want to adopt children or if I'm trying to fill a void from something I didn't get from when I was a child. I mean, I don't want to go through the process to adopt when I'm not emotionally equipped with the skills and tools to be able to nourish them in a way that creates a sense of wholeness."

She paused and gazed at me.

"Sorry for unloading all that onto you. I hope it's not too much."

I smiled at her, allowing a moment of silence for the patterns of star constellations to emerge in front of me. There was a feeling of cosmic order. This woman was about to enter into a portal of expansive self-illumination.

"There's so much wonder awaiting you," I said, smiling.

Over the next six months, Julie would allow herself to move through the process of identifying and dismantling her belief that she shouldn't want more than she already had, along with old beliefs about family that no longer served her. Because she lived in New York, our sessions were online. In these sessions, she discovered that she had been anchored by an early belief that she was not good enough, not perfect enough, and unworthy. She would pull on the tangle of emotions and shame and guilt to discover a deep-seated fear that she wasn't strong enough to add more members to her "family" experience. She wanted insurance that she could provide a healthy and whole foundation to raise her kids in a loving, nurturing environment and have the tools to be the emotionally supportive mother she'd never had. This enabled her to bring more awareness to her past family experience and how it still triggered her. Some of the threads she identified were:

- Her parents fought and then pretended nothing had happened.
- Strength was displayed as void of emotion.
- Her sister used her sexual energy to manipulate and hurt others. On several occasions, she felt her sister had violated boundaries by giving her husband private cards and gifts. She felt sad because she didn't know how to have healthy boundaries with her family of origin.
- She loved her sister, yet she was constantly comparing herself to her and didn't trust her at all.
- She truly loved her family, yet she knew this wasn't the family legacy she wanted to experience anymore or pass down.
- She had thought that honoring herself meant she would lose her family, and she didn't want that.

Julie deeply desired to trust and nurture herself while remaining open and able to love others. She didn't know how to let herself feel grief, as it had always felt weak. She was right: Self-care did need to be more than a mani-pedi.

Before she could discern if her longing to adopt was simply an attempt to patch up her wounded past, Julie needed to shed layers of shame, guilt, and unworthiness. She needed to release trying to be someone she wasn't. Her process involved a fair amount of clearing clutter, activating her own inner healthy discernment, re-evaluating her family dynamics, and upgrading her communication skills with family.

- Julie ended up adopting two children, saving them from a potentially life-threatening situation with drug-addicted parents.
- She kept the job she loved and got the help she needed to care for the kids by hiring an assistant to help with cooking, cleaning, and household needs.
- She opened a yoga studio, which fulfilled a dream she never even knew she had.
- She was happier than she'd ever been and felt that her relationships were able to nourish her spirit and support her on her highest path.
- She had learned how to cue into the signs that she was letting her energy leak and knew how to call it back in.
- She harnessed her own energy and became fully committed to who she was becoming while still honoring where she had been.

If you're thinking Julie somehow gained tools and abilities that had previously eluded her, you're right. Yet, with the right insight and tools, the growth she was able to experience in her life was limitless, and, you can experience the same Illumination.

OWNING YOUR DESIRE

Starting this work can sometimes feel like you are standing in the center of a maze. You may feel stuck, or trapped, or have no idea which direction to go in. By admitting this stuck feeling and having the desire to not feel this way anymore, you open yourself to receiving support.

Like Julie, many of us have been taught that our desires are bad. Heaven forbid that you have amazing, earth-shattering, huge, passionate desires! Desire has been given a bad rap. In reality, it's nothing more than your soul's way of guiding you to clarity. To own and work to fulfill your desires is to place your feet on the path back to your purpose.

You may not be able to identify any desires at first. Sometimes it's enough to start with what you know you don't want. No more of that dead feeling. Like being an impostor in your own life. No more panic or anxiety. Then, perhaps, you'll find an opening into your good desires. What does an amazing, full, vibrant life look like? (Hint: Nothing, absolutely nothing, is too big.) It doesn't need to make sense. In fact, if it does make sense, you're probably not thinking big enough yet.

NO RIGHT WAY

I know how it feels to be broken, at a complete loss of how to move forward, and yanked back and forth by the moorless dangers of a seemingly purposeless life. Over a couple of decades, I traveled continents and incorporated rituals and practices from various tribes and cultures into my energetic toolbox. I'm a big believer that what works for one person won't necessarily work for another. This is not cookie cutter work. Yet there are some commonalities as well. Here are a couple of touchstones to help you shape a sacred container for safe transformation.

CALL IN SACRED SPACE

Invoking sacred space is an energetic invitation to take your shoes off and leave the busy world behind. When you call in sacred space, life slows down and you gain new perspective. You create a field of protection and allow your heart to open. This will release you from your current thought processes and let your mind relax.

THE WAY OUT IS THROUGH

Often when people begin this work, they seem as if they are encased in concrete, like a huge block with no cracks in it. As they develop a willingness to admit that they're feeling stuck, the concrete begins to crack so the light can shine out. Cracks can scare people to death. But it is the death of living a life encased in concrete that can expand into unlimited potential. They can sense that they are nearing the point of no-turning-back and may hesitate on the edge, afraid to stay where they are yet afraid to change. This is when I tell them that the only way out is through...and that they'll have support on their journey. Let's look at how Jessica made it through.

"I have the same issue with men over and over again," she said, her voice gentle. "Men don't respect me." She paused, shifted her position and her voice became bubbly. "As soon as I begin to show interest in a man, I feel high, like I can soar into the limitless sky. I feel like I'm attracted to men that seem to go into hyper-drive to woo me with gifts, attention, and affection, and lots of flirting. It's so fun."

And then, her shoulders sank into her body, as if creating a cage around her heart for protection. Tears welled up and she put her hand on her throat as if to soothe the pain that was bubbling out.

"But then they ignore me and I feel empty. I don't want to beg for attention and yet, after a while, I feel starved for even a passing sweet glance. I'm so sad, I want to find true love but I just feel like a helium balloon that gets punctured and becomes deflated...useless."

I thanked her for trusting and sharing with me and asked if she would be open to a few reflections.

"Yes," she whispered, nodding and reaching for a tissue.

"Where do you feel the presence of 'useless' in your body?"

She placed her hands right below her heart and rubs her solar plexus.

"What does it feel like to feel useless?"

"Like I just care and no one else cares back, it feels painful." She closed her eyes, wiped them, and found where this pain lives inside of her body. She kept her hands on the same spot, rubbing her solar plexus.

I suggested that she address the pain directly and ask it, "What are you here to teach me?"

"Let your pain do the talking instead of having your mind answer the questions," I guided.

Her face distorted and she seemed to dive right into the pain. I guided her to ask the pain when she first felt it.

She flashes back to when she was a young girl. She was babysitting her younger sister Abby, who was four years old or so and asking her to clean her room. It was Jessica's responsibility to make sure the house was clean, and she had to teach Abby how to clean up her own mess. But Abby screamed in protest and Jessica told her she would take her teddy bear until the room was clean.

"Abby was screaming when my father came home from work. She kept saying, 'Jessica has my teddy bear, she won't give it back to me.' I was standing in the hall watching in slow motion as he lunged at me. It felt like the hallway walls were collapsing in on me. My father picked me up by twisting his fist into my shirt, right here."

She rubbed her solar plexus again.

"Everything was as if in slow motion. He hurled me against the back wall of the hall, and I collapsed on the floor. I couldn't breathe."

She gasped.

"Pain, what are you teaching me?"

"Men are violent. People I love hurt me the most. Don't trust. Be on guard at all times. I am bad. I'm a failure. My dad hates me. I'm unlovable, and anyone I love could turn on me at any moment, wait for it."

"Wow, those are pretty powerful contracts," I said. "Would you like to keep those in your body, or would you like to create space for new contracts in your body?"

"Yes, please, I want new contracts."

She pulls at the contracts she's been holding tight inside her.

"Now you can burn them," I told her. "Watch each one turn to ash, let the fire burn every last shred of pain associated with this memory. What new contracts would you like to write?"

"I am lovable. I am amazing. I trust myself. I love myself. I give and receive unconditional love. I am worthy. I am safe."

"Where in your body do you want to place these new contracts?" I asked. She pulled them into her solar plexus. Her posture opened. Her chest moved forward. She smiled; her eyes still closed. Her body readjusted and she looked as if she was sitting on a throne, regal and calm.

"Pain sometimes takes on a new shape after you've written new contracts," I suggested. "What's happening for you right now?

"The pain is a luminous being. It's me as a little girl."

"She's ready to come back to live inside your body," I suggested. "She misses you and wants you to take care of her."

"How do I take care of you?" Jessica asked the being. And the answer came to her.

"Spend time in nature, sing, dance, enjoy life, write, share stories, forgive dad."

With her newly expanded awareness, Jessica could see her father as an angry man without the tools to deal with his anger. His rage wasn't about her, and it wasn't her fault. She felt love from her father even though that time his actions were not loving. She could see her father as a human being who made a big mistake. She reclaimed the parts of herself that felt unlovable. She thanked him and set them both free of the story. There's a new space for a fresh relationship with herself, her father, and everyone to whom she relates.

Jessica sighed and glowed even brighter. A power animal enters her mind's eye, she said.

A dove. She asked the dove why he's here. He tells her he is here to collect any remnants of old contracts and the feeling of uselessness. She feels a sense of residual fatigue ease out of her and offers it to the bird. The dove flies off.

I grabbed my singing bowl and chimed it. Jessica rubbed her throat and a sound comes out, a singing tone. She harmonized with the sound of the bowl. She began to sing.

She opened her eyes and her face looked different. Renewed. She walked over to the mirror, looked, and said, "I feel like myself. I don't know how to describe it, but I feel at home inside myself. I always wanted to sing, and I just couldn't. I feel open now."

Several months later, Jessica met her soulmate and falls madly in love. When they married, she sang at her wedding. Today she is happily married with two children and has a positive and growing relationship with her father.

EXERCISES TO IGNITE YOUR LIGHT

How luminous is your life? Like Jessica, do you have songs you want to sing to express your own irresistible self? You, who lives your destiny as you embody your powerful mission. You, who's aligned with right thinking, right loving and right action for your highest good and the highest good of all. If you're not living deliciously, try out one of these starter exercises. For meditations on each of these exercises, and access to additional miracle-working energy medicine, visit **www.luxmecollective.com.**

- **Spark your flame.** Remember that concrete block that represents a person's energy in the beginning of an illumination process? When that concrete block is solid, no light gets out. Imagine that your personal concrete is somehow light and flaky. Chunks can break off. Cracks can emerge. Instead of looking at these cracks in horror, I'm here to tell you the cracks reveal what's beneath personas and self-illusions. They break your old stories into pieces so you can tell a bigger, broader story of yourself and others. A story that allows even the hard things in our lives to be kind to us. What do your cracks reveal? Is there a gold river running underneath? A liquid light that shines out?

- **Stoke your courage.** Recall a moment in which you were coura-geous. Blow on the embers of that moment and feel the warmth of your own courage. Let the light that radiates out from you illuminate your surroundings. What can you see now with your courage glow-ing that was previously in darkness? If something particular calls your attention, bring a glowing ball of courage with you and walk closer to whatever it is and shine the light of your expanding aware-ness on it. Does it transform before your eyes?
- **Unleash your radiance.** One way to access your deepest knowing and live your life beyond your wildest imaginings is to surround yourself with beauty. Select an object and place it in your home in a position of sacred reverence. It may be a lit candle or a blooming flower. It may be a dandelion or a twisted piece of wood. Whatever speaks to you and softens your heart space. Take a few minutes each day to notice the beauty in your object, allow yourself to feel the beauty of your natural environment, of your sensual ripening, of your fearless wholeness, of your open heart and divine connection. Enjoy this window into your own radiant beauty.

MIRACLES ARE REAL

Join me in saying welcome to the fullness of your own life—a life where the beauty of your luminous self and the velvety softness of your open heart unfurls. You are awakening to your truth at this very important time in the great story. You can transform your life completely. It's as possible for you as it was for the women you read about here.

It's time to access your gifts, align with your own convictions, and share your gifts with the world.

"Let us temper our criticism with kindness.
None of us comes fully equipped."

—Carl Sagan

When you're ready to get in touch with your true nature—that spark of divinity within you—**Jamie Brandenberg** is here to support your evolution. A lover of sacred traditions, Jamie has spent decades traveling continents and incorporating rituals and practices from various tribes and cultures. She shapes this fertile ground into sacred containers for her clients' safe transformations, guiding them through a process of connecting with their own inner wisdom and owning their truth. Jamie is founder of LUXME Collective, an organization that

brings people together in support of each other's full radiance. Jamie is a coach, published author, international speaker, mother, friend, and wife. You can reach Jamie at **www.luxmecollective.com.**

Special Gift

CALLING IN SACRED SPACE

When your body lacks grounding, your mind is racing, or your heart snaps shut like a clam, use this recording to create a safe container for your energetic unfolding. When you invoke sacred space, you expand in all six directions. The physical plane of North, East, South and West, the depth of the soul sphere, and the soaring heights of the spirit all fuse to help you gain valuable insight and assistance from your guides.

The practice of calling in sacred space creates a field of protection that grounds your body, calms your mind, and opens your heart to unimaginable miracles. Use it wherever you are, whenever you need it. For a free audio recording that will walk you through the process of calling in sacred space, visit **www.luxmecollective.com/sacredspace.html.**

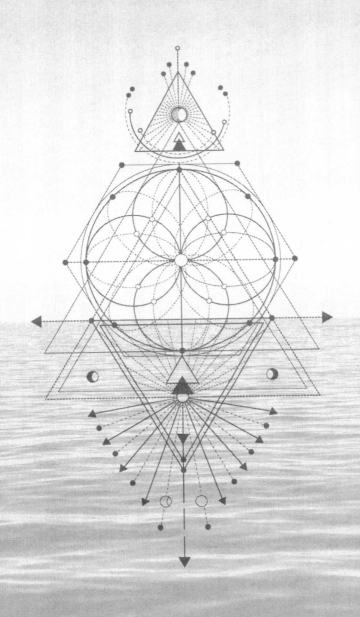

A New Bloom:
Navigating the Alchemy of Life

BY FAYE CALLAWAY

I made it.

Through all of the moments when I didn't think I could keep going, through all of the tears and the rage and pain, through all of the doubt and insecurity... I passed through the initiation of my own personal transcendence. I walked the fires of trauma and swam through oceans of despair to finally arrive at the place I have been yearning for: the place of my own. The place where I stand in my sovereignty and my magic. The place of my true power and my freedom.

And there was no other way to get here, no path around, no way out but through. This is the labyrinth of life. This is the vortex.

"Through dangers untold and hardships unnumbered, I have fought my way here to the castle beyond the Goblin City to take back the child that you have stolen. For my will is a strong as yours, and my kingdom is as great... You have no power over me."

—*Labyrinth*, 1986, Sony Pictures

In alchemy, this labyrinth walk is referred to as the Dark Phase, encompassing the processes of *Calcination* and *Dissolution*. It's an inner journey represented by the dark forests of fairy tales and the many tales of the underworld. But why do I bring up these strange names? Why does that even matter?

Because this is the process that must occur to reach true expansion and happiness and to finally clear anything standing in the way of a life of self-actualized desire. If we don't walk these fires and release these old patterns and energies, we stay stuck and we never achieve the culmination of our potential here on Earth—we never bloom. Fear not, my Sisters. Everything you ever wanted is on the other side of your pain. Open the door to your healing and leap into your salvation!

You are not alone. I am here to tell you that you are supported and loved. All of us who are undergoing deep transformation and shifts for the betterment of ourselves and the planet are here for you. We do this together. And here, I share my story of how I got through, in the hopes that it will help my Sisters get through their darkest times. With deep love and humble gratitude, I share what the Goddess has shared with me; I share her wisdom and her alchemy.

ALCHEMY

The Black Phase of my Transformation—the processing and release of trauma after trauma after trauma—has resulted in a new chapter of my life. I am now lighter, and the feeling is ecstatic, like joy combined with a new passion for experiences and a drive to engage in life. It's a new bloom. *A radiant emergence!* In some ways, it even feels like the birth of a star within my soul, like a true cosmic connection has forged within.

This, finally, is the fun part of alchemy.

So, what is alchemy? To most it brings up images of medieval men with strange tubes and flasks and weird creations. To those who fear it, alchemy is creepy and dangerous. To others, its dismissed as fantasy. Nothing could be further from the truth, however. Alchemy is not any of those things. Alchemy is life. Alchemy is freedom.

The first three steps of alchemy are Calcination, Dissolution, and Separation. There are seven steps total, however currently I am in the third step,

Separation—having just recently emerged from many years of Calcination/ Dissolution. These were years of delving into the pain and examining it and releasing over and over...years of triggers and traumas and lessons. Years of crying and grieving and letting go.

Years that saved my life.

Before that, I had been frozen and fearful of examining my own pain. Standing in my own fires, my life dripping around me as I struggled to maintain. It took *so* much energy, *so* much life force. It was draining. Exhausting. It was slowly killing me as I continued to numb myself from the pain through my own unhealthy patterns.

Then, something happened.

Love came into my life and with it came a great awakening. I felt my entire body shifting from my very cells into my consciousness and my beingness. It was a total shift, a transformation. And with it, my entire life changed. My heart was somehow...opened. I woke up and couldn't deny the pain any longer. I was no longer numb to the fires of Calcination. I was in the damn fires, burning up alive. I needed to get it under control. I needed massive change.

I suddenly left a nineteen-year relationship that had become extremely disabling and toxic, leaving behind my entire identity that was formed during that relationship, and then having to let go of everything that had been attached to it. It was devastating and horrible, but the magic of the new love I had found sustained me through it. However, I had not yet even begun the true process of Dissolution. I didn't even know what release and surrender was truly like until I lost that new love to mental illness and then shortly afterward my long-term ex-partner died. At that point, my entire world fell apart. I was completely lost, not even sure of who I was anymore. Loss, pain, and death seemed like the only things in life anymore.

I suffered for some time. I suffered because I did not yet realize that I didn't need to. And then I was reminded:

Pain is inevitable, but suffering is optional.

By being willing to examine myself, releasing energies and patterns I no longer needed, I was able to address my trauma and, most importantly, begin to engage in a loving relationship with myself. I started by removing the people who judged me unfairly and I surrounded myself with people who see me with love in their eyes, who witness me. I also relieved myself of caring for the rest of the world. I recognized that I was actually taking power away from *them* while draining *myself* in the process. Everyone has their own connection to a higher power, or Source—the One Heart. And everyone has their own unique blocks that keep them from fully embodying that Source. These blocks can only be released by ourselves by choice, not by anyone else. It is the law of Free Will. And when we violate that law by trying to remove other people's blocks, we are no longer fully connected to our own Source and we falter while at the same time preventing the other person from fully engaging with their own inner power. We cannot feel fully empowered while we are unplugged. We must each devote ourselves to our own Source connection, whatever that looks like.

The process of alchemy is not changing what's around me, it's altering what's in me to become more in tune with what's around me and thus allowing me to more easily align to what I desire. Because all that I desire I am, it's literally in the molecules themselves. But to become what I desire I must dissolve my attachments to anything in the way. This is the second step of alchemy. Life itself takes care of the first, that which we call Calcination. The Calcination is the fire. The tragedy. The traumatic events. The things of life we all fear but which are what free us from the illusion of our powerlessness.

The dissolution, or dissolving, however, is optional. We may avoid it if we choose, by numbing ourselves to the process and therefore opting out of the game. But if we trust the process, knowing that real magic is held in the mystery itself, we accept the quest. We rise to the challenge and, in doing so, in examining ourselves in crisis and in turmoil, we come to see the power we hold within. For it is only through the fires that the sword of inner power can be born. We ourselves become the crucible, burning away all that we no longer need. And then, we forge a sword that is unstoppable in its ability to cut through illusion.

THE SWORD AND RITUAL OF SELF-HONOR

Symbols allow for greater connection to energies. One of the greatest symbols of power is the sword, an object that connects us to the energies of truth, wisdom, discernment, and clarity. Feel your inner sword, see the sword rise within you. Feel it cut away everything you no longer need. Feel it shatter all obstacles in your way. Feel it in your hand, rising over your head, and slashing through your fears.

The only way to cut ourselves loose from the spiral of destruction that gathers around us is by stilling the breath, finding that inner power, and cutting through the bullshit. Use the sword to remind you to stand tall and see clearly. Shed all doubt. Know that you can choose always for your highest good simply by setting that intention and then following up with loving wise action. This is the way of The Queen.

Stand tall with your inner sword, Queen. The world has only begun to know your true power.

THE RITUAL

There's something that happens when a woman clears space for herself, when she extracts herself from the chaos that inevitably swarms around her, attracted to her very wild essence. When she stands still. When she takes a breath. When she hears only her own breath.

Listening.

It is a sound of Magic. A sound beckoning her to go deeper, to go inside. The sound that calls her to her own soul, her own cosmic inner rabbit hole.

This is the way to the eye of the hurricane. Through stillness. And breath. And an incredible love for oneself. A love that roots. A love that sprouts and rises, tall and strong within us. A love that eventually blossoms, straight from the inner heart.

It is a love that saves us. A love that will never betray us. A love that holds us up from the very core of our being-ness, against any odds. And every one of us has it.

Stand still. Really still. So still you can feel your own cells vibrating.

Now breathe.

There it is.

Can you feel it?

The strength coming up from the Earth, slowly spiraling up your feet, legs, hips, and up. It dances around you. Feel it pool in your chest. A literal wellspring of inner strength resides within your own heart. It is Her gift to you, as Her daughter. And no one can ever take it away from you, Sister.

So just breathe, Sister, and focus your heart. Radiant, clear, beacon that you are. There is no lie that can convince you, no manipulation that can get past you, no deceit than can attach to you.

You are a being of true wisdom and divine insight.

You are Magic. You are Imagined and you are Imagination and you are in the Image. I, Mage.

Standing in this place of power, go deeper. Breathing up the center channel of your being, imagine a light cord rising up from Earth, straight out of the rocks itself, and up the spine. Feel the light cord rise all the way up, to the top of the head. Then, the light begins to shift and solidify, the energy pulling inward toward your center like there is a magnetic line that goes from head down to your spinal tip. Sit, lie, or stand very still as you imagine this. Sense it focus within, like a liquid metal rod of light. It shifts and swirls, in iridescent colors of silvered mercurial substance. This is the One Thing as it forms the object of your desire, and of your imagination, becoming the inner Sword. The energetic quicksilver forms a hilt, and a blade, and the cross of the handle falls right at the heart, the center of knowing, where all wisdom and love radiate out. The power of the sword combined with the magic of the radiant heart creates the glory of the inner Alchemical Excalibur that now resides within you.

INVOCATION

With this sword I clear-cut my forest of doubts and fears and reveal the truth of the garden of the One Heart within me. I cut the belief that I owe this world my soul, for my soul is this world. I cut the belief that I am not good enough, for I am All. I cut away the fear of standing in my power, as I am The Power. I cut away any doubt that I have the power to change this world through the force of love that flows through my heart because I am the Love. I cut away the belief that I was ever separated from The One and I acknowledge that I am a sovereign Queen in service to the One Heart. RAHU RAKAN and So it is!

Now, write *your* Invocation. Wield your sword of truth, Queen!

THE GODDESS

She has a message for you:

> *Unravel the cords that bind you and embrace all that surrounds you.*
> *Create the space for inner grace.*

Ariadne's voice comes to me, reaching through the millennia to speak her truth to her daughters. She is here for us. She is our thread, our guide, our usher into our own shadow. She is a gatekeeper and the one who guards the chamber of our soul and the power of our sword. She is our ally, our mother, our sister, and ourselves. She is our *shakti* and our wisdom, our serpent and our thread.

She is known as "Mistress of the Labyrinth", "the Great Goddess", and "The Potnia". Ariadne is often remembered as the woman who assisted Theseus in the Greek story of the Minotaur. Although she is a key element in assisting us in facing our inner self, our beast, she is far more than these stories let on. Ariadne was a goddess unto her own right. A high priestess, a guardian of secrets and the realms of mystery. Keeper of inner portals and outer illusions, it is said that the Minoan celebrations of Ariadne and her Maenads would last days, maybe weeks, as her worshipers danced their way to ecstatic liberation. Thus, when what you need is guidance, she is a most worthy Goddess to have by your side.

ARIADNE

(From *Ariadne's Thread* by Shekhinah Mountainwater)

In the deepening twilight
She stands
Just inside the entrance
To her cave,
Beckoning.

"Come," she softly calls
"Follow me."
"But I am afraid," you tell her.
"I fear I will be lost in there,
And they say that there are Minotaurs."

You peer into the labyrinth
Behind her,
The twisting passages
Winding away
To nothing...

Out here the familiar world
Crashes on.
The Sea of Sexism,
the City of Doom.
She lifts her proud dark gaze in scorn
"'Tis there one meets the Minotaur"

In the Shadow gleams her crescent crown
A snake stirs at her breast
And in her hand she holds the Thread
Unraveling a strand
And offering...

Will you come
Oh my sister
Will you come?

Faye Callaway is a Mystical Priestess, author, Primal Goddess-Muse-Beloved Genuine Ginger Witchcrafter, and Priestess Presence and 13 Moon Initiate. Faye is a devoted initiate of the Goddess of Love in the lineage of the Magdalene and has spent a large portion of her life studying various paths of mysticism, shamanism and magic, including alchemy which is itself the parent of various scientific and spiritual paths.

Through her studies, Faye has observed herself transform in both the inner and the outer realms. Her purpose is to remind others who they really are. Through the path of love, she vows to touch as many hearts as possible and help awaken humanity to its amazing potential and extraordinary capabilities.

Learn more at **www.mystichealix.com** and **www.fayecallaway.com**.

Special Gift

INVOKE YOUR INNER POWER WITH THE ELEMENTS! A RITUAL FOR WILD-ASS WITCHES

With this ritual, you will use the elements to create a crucible for the energetic alchemy of calling in your true heart's desires.

Access here: **www.fayecallaway.com/setsail**

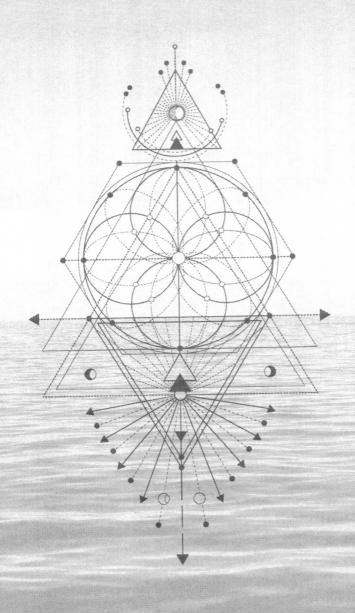

The Intuitive Chef and Her Kitchen Alchemy: Crafting the Recipe for a Life of Purpose

BY LAUREN D'AGOSTINO

What do you want to be when you grow up?

As a child, I often avoided answering that question. Unlike other kids at daycare, I didn't fantasize about being a famous singer, dancer, or super-hero. Unlike my friends at school, I wasn't totally obsessed with dressing up as a princess, cowgirl, or movie star. And unlike my high school class-mates, I wasn't dedicated to playing the same sport season after season with the hope of someday becoming a professional. However, I knew exactly what I wanted to be when I grew up. Unfortunately, I always felt insecure and kind of embarrassed to share it.

I was busy daydreaming about owning a restaurant and hosting mag-nificent dinner parties. I would fantasize about serving a carefully selected menu to my most delightful friends and customers, who would admire my seemingly effortless ability to prepare such a delicious spread. I would craft beautiful menus from simple ingredients and share delicious dishes in a warm and inviting space that people flocked to. I loved cooking, eat-ing, art, and design, and being together at the table. It was the only way I knew to express love and appreciation, and I craved hearing how incredi-ble my food was because it made me feel appreciated, accepted, admired, and most importantly, loved.

As immersed as I was in these fantasies, I never had the children's version of anything when it came to the kitchen. No Easy-Bake Oven. No plastic kitchen playset. And definitely no ordering off the silly kids' menu. At two years old, I was playing on the floor of our kitchen with pots and pans and a bag of flour. I had an adorable apron of my own and had started a cookbook collection as soon as I could read. At four, I was ordering my own meals off the same menu as the adults at restaurants. As I got older, I asked for kitchen gadgets and cookie cutters for Christmas and birthdays and had my own subscriptions to cooking magazines. When we were out to dinner, I loved to "get lost" finding the bathroom just to get a peek inside the kitchen. My mom would take me to cooking demonstrations in Boston and, even though I was always the youngest foodie in attendance, I always felt like I belonged.

As a young and aspiring professional chef, I watched the Food Network every day after school before starting my homework. I would pretend that I had my own cooking show as I followed a printed recipe from my culinary idols, after watching them prepare it on their show. I'd gather all my ingredients in little ramekins, just like they did, and talk to myself while following their every instruction.

I loved to play restaurant with real food in our dining room. Even if I served a simple grilled cheese, my set-up was over the top, complete with fancy folded napkins and a fake guest check. I would welcome anyone who was hungry—the babysitter, the cleaning lady, the mailman—simply because I wanted to delight people with food and serve love on a plate.

At nine years old, I knew I wanted to be a chef.

I would stay up late reading cookbooks cover to cover like they were novels. I was completely fascinated by these lists of food that somehow combined in a perfect way to create something new and totally different. As I watched meals being prepared on television, or read the instructions in a book, I could taste the experience each step of the way. I developed a talent for taste, which often worked against me as I set unrealistically high expectations for every meal I ate.

Always looking for a place to fit in and feel comfortable in my surroundings, I was an identity chameleon, but I felt a sense of belonging in this world of culinary arts, service, hospitality, and creativity. I explored any opportunity to turn this natural curiosity and talent into a career. I went to culinary camps, food tastings, and cooking demonstrations, always sitting in the front or volunteering to assist the instructor.

My recent reflection on all personal and professional experiences to this point has helped me understand my legacy. These experiences were part of my journey to prepare me to teach people to create nourishing and seasonal meals so they could then live their legacy, creating healthy traditions for generations. Learning to connect to my intuition and channeling this individual guidance from a sacred place of love, deep respect for the physical body, and in collaboration with nature's rhythms is the gift that I have been blessed to receive. I am so passionate about intuitive cooking that this philosophy is part of my coaching process when working with clients in their first few steps of transitioning to a plant-based diet.

Isn't it amazing that the sun shines on our beautiful planet Earth and that its energy is used by the many plants that grow here to produce the most delicious and nutritious food available, mostly without us having to do a thing? I found it incredibly powerful to realize this and to connect with my food this way. You become, quite literally, whatever it is that you eat. Your body uses the contents of your meals to regenerate, repair, and revitalize itself, and it can only do this properly if given the fuel and nutrients that support this process.

When I was blessed to realize that what I was eating was harming me, I was realistic with how I would transition to a plant-based diet in a sustainable way.

I had been a vegetarian for a year in college, after taking a few sustainability classes at the University of Massachusetts in Amherst. I was so inspired that I challenged myself to only eat foods that were grown or produced within a 100-mile radius of our crunchy college town. I was also very physically active as a way to escape some toxic relationships and was really starting to lean on the control and stability that I felt within a vegetarian diet. This was a very challenging time for me personally and socially, so it's really no surprise that I developed a bit of orthorexia—a condition that includes symptoms of obsessive behavior and anxiety in pursuit of a healthy diet. My first round of vegetarianism came to a screeching halt at the end of the summer before going back to campus for senior year.

I challenged myself again, but this time the stakes were higher and bit more rooted in vanity—I tried veganism for the summer and was so crazy about reading labels. I ate a ton of scrambled tofu and relied on vegan junk foods that were starting to show up on supermarket shelves. I drove myself insane and was hyper emotional, had developed a soy allergy, and was as thin as I had ever been. My family and friends were concerned, and I eventually made my way back to animal products, vowing to stick to ethical sourced products. I realize now that the intention for changing my lifestyle back then was equally rooted in ethics and sustainability, as well as vanity and control. I had set the wrong intention, so of course it was not sustainable—or even healthy!

My intention this time, however, was to fully embody a vegan plant-based lifestyle that was in sync with the cycles of the seasons and was health-promoting. This included food, of course, but also other lifestyle components such as essential oils, astrology, and a spiritual practice that resonated with me. I knew that all these components of a holistic lifestyle were important for me to feel a deeper connection and sense of fulfilled purpose that I'd been searching for ever since being asked the question *"What do you want to be when you grow up?"*

I began this journey with the food because I felt comfortable and capable in a culinary world, and because food is the foundation of everything that we are. It took a conscious effort to reevaluate my diet and actively choose what made sense for me each step of the way. I reset my mind to be patient and kind with myself during this process and valued this commitment and connection to my intention. This was critical and, at times, not easy, because I was working long days as a pastry chef for Disney and restaurant server at Cafe Tu Tu Tango in Orlando, constantly surrounded by delicious temptations.

The process took about three months to achieve the lifestyle I wanted, and since then, I've been able to sustain it for more than four years. The first step for me was to eliminate red meat, which felt very doable because I never cared much for it anyway. I got comfortable in a lifestyle that did not include any red meat or meat products. When I went grocery shopping, I simply skipped over this section and happily noticed that my bill reduced. When I went out to eat, I had an easier time making decisions on what to order, something that had always been difficult for me. I knew right away which items were not a fit for my lifestyle, thereby reducing my options. I lived within this dietary framework until red meat became something that I did not miss, did not crave, and did not think about.

The next step was to remove chicken and all other meat. This was slightly more challenging, though not difficult because I held that intention I had set so close to my awareness every single day. I thought about everything I had learned about the poor quality of the foods I was working to eliminate and what happened in my body when I consumed them. I learned to love fresh vegetables and salads and enjoyed stepping into a vegetarian lifestyle again. The pros were beginning to outweigh the cons, and I was discovering so many new foods and cuisines that it was exciting rather than limiting. I lived within this dietary framework until all meat and poultry became something that I did not miss, did not crave, and did not think about.

After that, becoming a full-time vegetarian by eliminating fish was a breeze because I had already fallen so in love with fruits and vegetables and had started to notice changes in my physical body. I was sleeping better, my skin was more radiant, my digestion improved, and I recovered faster in between workouts. When I was cooking at home, preparation and clean-up had become so easy because I wasn't using any raw meat. Realizing that I could continue enjoying these benefits by also cutting out fish was a no-brainer. When I went grocery shopping, my trips were faster because I had less retail space to explore. I discovered some amazing produce markets, farm stands, and other local vendors at farmers' markets. When I was dining out, I knew to look right for the vegetarian section. I had become more comfortable asking for what I wanted if any modifications were required to meet my needs. I lived within this dietary framework until being vegetarian was something that I could own, something that I enjoyed, and something that I excelled at.

A few weeks or months later, I took a big step in my journey by removing the dairy and eggs from my diet, which for many people is the hardest part, myself included. When I was making choices at the market and at home, I avoided these ingredients because it was easy to simply not buy them. When I was dining out, however, I still chose the vegetarian option and if dairy and eggs were part of the dish, I was more lenient and found that I was not yet comfortable requesting a change to a menu item. I had not fully stepped into my ownership of a vegan plant-based diet, but I was satisfied with where I was. The decision to be kind with myself was a personal choice that really helped me feel into this new way of eating and living in a way that felt right for me.

Once I started to see the difference in my skin and energy, I knew that it was time to be a full-time plant-based vegan, but by then I was ready and I still knew why this was so important to me. I could really feel the affect it was having on my health. I was also lucky to live in Orlando where there is a large vegetarian and vegan community. It was at this point that I felt comfortable sharing details about my diet with people who asked; before that, I kept it my business, because it was my business after all.

When you change your diet, it is important to stay focused on your intentions and the reasons for the change. Do not listen to outside influence or broadcast your new lifestyle to friends and family who will try to take you off track. I know how hard it can be to keep information to ourselves about how our food choices impact our health, especially after watching any of the health films that have hit the mainstream. When I was able to lead by example instead of preaching my diet to anyone with ears, I had an easier time sharing what I had learned. People were interested and wanted to know my secrets, and they genuinely took interest in what I had experienced. Once I understood that everybody is different, I came to appreciate everyone's individual journey. I started to become curious about people's reasons for being vegan and the types of new foods that they enjoyed and old foods that they missed.

The transition to living plant-based should be full of new discoveries for your taste buds and your body. You can eat whatever you like, but you will find over time that you will actively choose the healthier options, because intuitively it feels right. I still reach for recipes and cookbooks for inspiration from time to time, but with a little practice, you will not need to measure every ingredient. You won't need to keep going back to the top of the recipe because you lost your place, again, and fear that you'll skip a step.

*What I practice and teach is cooking for real. Using real food,
enjoying real flavor, and having real fun.*

I have been cooking for more than twenty-five years, which is almost all of
my life, and during that time I have studied many methods of food preparation, techniques, and cuisines. Like many home cooks and professional
chefs, I used to depend on recipes to navigate the preparation of my food.
I used to have sticky notes and index cards sticking out haphazardly out
of every cookbook I owned. But I always felt overwhelmed and guilty that
the recipes would hardly ever be prepared. Cooking is something we all
used to do intuitively, but like so many things in life, when we see someone
else doing a better job than we do, we begin to believe that we need to seek
instruction outside of ourselves.

*Cooking is a vital skill that anyone can master, and it's simpli-
fied when only plant-based ingredients are used. It becomes fun
again when creativity and intuition can flow.*

Perhaps I owe some of my confidence to formal culinary training and
the many types of food service jobs I have held, or from the hours spent
learning everything I could about food and cooking as a kid. Learning to
cook from a young age is one of the best blessings in my life. I believe that
knowing how to cook for yourself in a nourishing way is something that
every person should know how to do for themselves.

In this new age of self-care and holistic health, one concept that I believe
is an important piece of the foundation of a healthy lifestyle is the practice
of intuitive home cooking.

Trusting yourself in the kitchen while preparing your meals is one of the most liberating things we can experience. Realizing that we each know exactly what will fuel our bodies on any given day gives the power back to us, in a time when it seems that everyone is confused by the latest in nutritional science. Feeding ourselves with meals that have been prepared purposefully, mindfully, and with high vibrations of love and gratitude is a powerful form of self-care. Embracing your expertise for your unique nutritional needs is so empowering, but we can only get there by partnering with Mother Nature and living a plant-based lifestyle.

As I was working my way through the creation of a vegan plant-based and gluten-free cafe menu for a client, I came to realize that I have a special gift. It was kind of a shock, because this gift is rooted in something that feels so unlike the Lauren that I have accepted for most of my life.

After years of energetic turmoil and disharmony with my external environment, a very clear picture popped into my mind from what seemed to be out of nowhere. The Universe showed me the concept of intuitive cooking, a term I had never used or heard before. It was so clearly the perfect label for what it was that I was doing, both in business and in my personal practice. I was combining my classical training, childlike sense of wonder for food, and love of plants and colors to help me eat foods and create meals that were exactly what my body was calling for.

As I realized this, I felt such a sense of peace, reassurance, and comfort that I had discovered my unique position in the culinary space and in the world.

In this model of intuitive cooking, no recipes are used, no meal plans are written, no counting and calculating is involved, and no fad diets or particular philosophies are followed. We simply learn to master a few methods of meal preparation that are very basic and customizable, and we let our creativity shine as we pair different seasonings and ingredients together.

In this new framework, I have never felt so free in my home kitchen, and I have never been so inspired and excited to share these techniques and teachings. So many people think that plant-based cooking is hard and time consuming, or expensive and out-of-reach. I have found that it is actually easier, faster, more economical, and so much more accessible than the way that so many are preparing their meals.

Cooking should be a fun and joyful way to spend time with our families and friends. It should be full of adventure, wonder, and new experiences. Eating is primarily a way for us to survive, but it can and should be so much more. When we take responsibility for what we put into our bodies, new meaning is given to the phrase "good enough to eat."

Lauren D'Agostino is a private plant-based chef, intuitive cooking coach, and speaker sharing simple strategies for fast and flavorful plant-based cooking. She teaches clients her signature intuitive cooking methods to encourage and support cooks of any level in the first few steps of their transition to a plant-based diet. Inspired by her work as a professional vegan chef, the global consciousness shift, and her own transition into living a plant-based life, she is guiding others to create lasting habits by incorporating more plants, both on and off the plate.

Lauren believes that everyone could benefit from eating and using more plants and works with her clients to teach them new strategies for plant-based meal preparation and healthcare. She shares her meal prep tips and cooking style with others in engaging classes, workshops, and private instruction in home kitchens in New England and across the globe. She is also a doTERRA Wellness Advocate, sharing the power and flavor of pure essential oils, and is releasing a cookbook December 2019.

Lauren is a graduate of the Institute for Integrative Nutrition, the Isenberg School of Business at the University of Massachusetts Amherst, and the Patisserie & Baking Program at Le Cordon Bleu. She is the former Chef de Cuisine at Plantz Cafe in Dracut, Massachusetts. She can be reached at **www.laurendagostino.com.**

Special Gift

FREE SHOPPING GUIDE WITH INSTRUCTIONAL VIDEO, PLUS SAMPLE RECIPES FROM LAUREN'S COOKBOOK!

Download Lauren's shopping guide and get started building your own intuitive kitchen pantry. Once you've changed the way you shop, you'll want to learn what to do with the ingredients on the list. Watch the bonus how to video at **www.laurendagostino.com/set-sail.**

If you're into natural solutions with essential oils and want to get an advance copy of her first cookbook, Plant-Based Cooking with Essential Oils, visit **www.laurendagostino.com/eo-cookbook.** Need the oils? Get those at **my.doterra.com/cheflaurendagostino.**

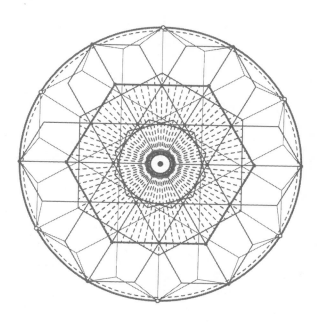

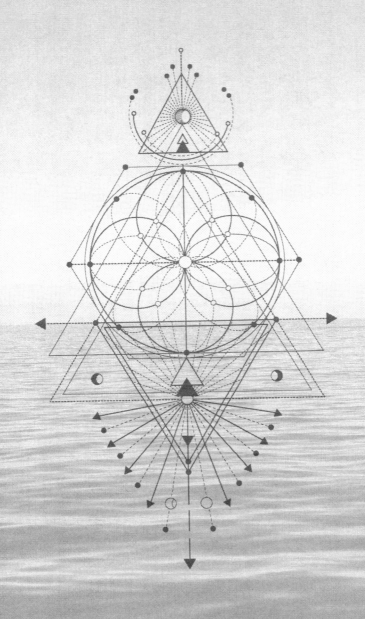

Communion with the Animals: The New Feminine Rising

BY ALLECIA EVANS

For most of my life growing up as a white Jewish girl in the Bronx I never really understood what the concept of Communion was about. I had no frame of reference of Oneness, as relationships in my household were based on fights, insecurity, lots of triangulations amongst family members, and a lot of unhealed emotional wounds and pain.

Of course, there were fun times and love in a dysfunctional way but there was a lot of hurtful actions that would leave scars for decades to come and scabs that would still need to be peeled off under my skin even four decades later. I had no concept of Communion from my religion as I saw people get dressed up on Friday evenings and Saturday mornings in their finest, say hello to people in their congregation and then gossip about the same people they were friendly with on Sundays. And my religion taught that God was above us in the sky, not dwelling with each of us as we lived.

The one thing I knew for sure was my love of animals. They were my one solace in a personal world that I could not seem to genuinely connect with and were always there for me to find my peace or a sense of comfort. I loved them so deeply but it would take me almost 25 years to begin to decode their teachings and deep wisdom in a way that would allow me to define and experience a new level of Holy Communion based on the Divine Feminine.

When my Mom asked me at five years old what I wanted to be when grew up I said, "A veterinarian because I want to help sick animals heal."

Eventually enough math and science were introduced that I realized I didn't have the aptitude for either of them to ever hope to make it into veterinary school.

So, I gave up that dream...or so I thought. Instead, what really happened was that I buried it deep within me. Many years later it would lead me down an unlikely path that would have me reclaiming my dream, yet it would look very different than I originally imagined.

After I graduated from high school and college, I entertained the thought of becoming a physical therapist. But, with the math and science involved, I instead became a fitness trainer at one of New York City's elite fitness clubs, Equinox. I loved fitness training. I was fascinated by the body and loved helping my clients achieve their health and fitness goals. I also loved feeling strong, fit, athletic, and healthy in my body.

During the first year of my fitness training career, I met a client named Andrea who was well versed in alternative health care and preventative medicine, and she understood about meditation, chiropractic care, acupuncture, qigong, and macro-nutrition. She was studying with a Chinese acupuncturist, was a single mom, and a was a fit model, raising her son in New York City.

As she became my client, she also became my "Spiritual Mom" so while I was teaching her how to strengthen her body she was actually teaching me how to connect with and strengthen my spirit.

I had never experienced meditation before. Honestly, I didn't even know what it was to sit and be quiet for more than thirty seconds unless I was exhausted from exercise. If you were to ask my mother to describe me, she would say "a flash of light." I was in...I was out...I was always moving around...maybe there was a part of me that was connected to myself, but there was definitely a part of me that absolutely was not.

Andrea began introducing me to a completely new world that allowed me to start to explore and discover what it was to actually be inside myself and to learn to feel what it's like to actually be peaceful and at one with myself.

One Christmas she gave me a gift certificate for an acupuncture session with Dr. Nan Lu, OMD. Despite my fear of needles, I began seeing Dr. Lu regularly for the next year. This led to me studying qigong with him every Friday at his American Taoist Healing Center in New York City.

I became deeply motivated to practice qigong. I actually fell in love with it. I dedicated one hour every morning and one hour every evening to it for three years straight without missing a single practice. Qigong—an ancient Chinese self-healing martial art—was my temple, my church, my mosque. It became and still is my sacred devotion for connecting with the energy of all life.

I didn't just practice on Friday evenings or go on Sunday mornings; even if I was on vacation, I woke up at 4:30 a.m. to practice. Qigong became my living breathing practice, as it was like taking an internal shower every day. I began reconnecting with the source energy of Mother Earth, which the Chinese refer to as The Tao, and which modern physics call The Quantum Energy Field, which permeates throughout every single aspect of life.

"Everything is energy. Everything is connected."

—The Tao

Qigong offered me a way of living that felt in harmony with all life. Through Traditional Chinese Medicine I learned that for more than five thousand years the Chinese have been studying and mapping the way the energy moves in and through the body and how to best keep it healthy by harmonizing it with nature. And they learned this system by studying animals in nature. I once asked Dr. Lu during a Friday class, "Once you have learned from the highest-level human teacher you can, and know that all human teachers have trace of ego, who do you study with next?"

He looked at me and said, "Nature, you study with nature. Nature is your highest teacher."

I will never forget one night around 11 p.m. while I was walking my dogs in the park across the street. I caught a whiff of the most amazing, fragrant flowers I had ever smelled. I'd lived in that neighborhood since I was nine years old and now at twenty-six had never smelled this on any summer before. This smell was something that I could only imagine would be found on an island like Hawaii. It made me feel so sensual and Goddess-like for the first time in my life. It was the scent of "Home."

I tried to wrap my head around it as the whole park was filled with the aroma, but for the life of me, I could only deduce that somehow I was being put in touch with a place I had never been to before and the flowers were sharing a divination of my future. This was the beginning of my body experiencing Communion before my mind would understand what was about to happen.

ALOHA!

During this time, my friend Diane phoned out of the blue to tell me about an "Animal Communication Retreat" with Mary Ann Simmonds on the Big Island of Hawaii.

Diane said that she knew I had to go. Her friend had been there the year before and her friend did qigong (like me), loved dolphins (like me), and was a fitness trainer (like me). There was something in Diane's voice that seemed to be coming from a higher state of conscious awareness, almost like spirit was talking to me through Diane.

I had no funds to go, but I called Mary Ann who informed me that the trip was full and yet after talking for twenty minutes, she said, "Yes, you must be here."

As I sat on my couch on an energy high, I remember sinking in and feeling the energy of myself being in Hawaii with the dolphins. I felt an open-hearted joy and excitement. It was from there that I requested that the Universe fund me and help me to get there.

I had purchased a ticket on a credit card at one price and checked in on the ticket the next day only to have the representative find me a ticket that cost $300 less. My dad stepped in to support me with the rest of the funds, and before I knew it, I had just taken the longest flight of my life to date, with ease, had helped a hyper-ventilating fellow passenger recover through breathwork, *and* landed on the island of my heart. And the very first thing I smelled was the unexplainable aroma of those flowers in the park that I had smelled a few years before.

How in the world did a scent from thousands of miles away that was separated by large oceans have the ability to be in that park that night? Through my qigong practice and the harmonizing of my energy field, somehow I was beginning to see that we can be in Communion with life no matter where we are.

THE ANIMALS STEP UP TO TEACH ME ABOUT ANOTHER VERSION OF COMMUNION

The retreat with Mary Ann was mind-blowing and heart-opening. She took us through many exercises during that week. But the one that I'll never forget was identifying our Amakua (according to Wikipedia, the appearance of an animal one regarded as an one regarded as an 'aumakua' was often believed to be an omen of good or ill).

As we proceeded through this exercise, we were told to go out and see what presents itself as our Amakua. I walked around for a minute and when I looked down on the ground just in front of me there was a perfectly preserved orange and black butterfly that had passed away. I brought it back and placed it on our retreat altar as our group reconnected.

During this time as our group was discussing each of our Amakuas, something began taking place within me. It reminded me of the energy that took place in the movie "The Lion King" when Rafiki threw the herbs in the air and realized the Simba was still alive. I began to feel this energy stirring inside of me that many people in the spiritual communities call "oneness."

I could feel this energy of oneness starting to run through my body and it felt as if my butterfly Amakua was coming alive and taking flight in my body. The experience made me feel like my body was part of that butterfly. It stayed with me all day and filled my sleep that evening. As I look back I see that my intellectual mind was releasing its intense hold on my gut brain, and I was simply coming back into balance with my instinctive knowing.

The next day we got up early to enjoy a lovely breakfast. It was my twenty-eighth birthday. I remembered having an odd feeling in my stomach as the dolphins hadn't been around for the first two days of the retreat. As seven of us women walked the ¼ mile to the beach from our house, our steps quickly picked up as we saw the dolphin fins in the bay. They were here! They had shown up for me on my special day. Talk about an epic birthday present! It felt like my heart was going to jump out of my chest with excitement and elation.

As we approached the water, it sounded like the dolphins were pretty far out. Even though I was a lifeguard in high school I didn't really feel completely confident about how far I would be able to swim. I felt the dolphins kept going further and further out, so I came toward shore a little closer and I saw a little white fuzzy ball (which I hoped was not poisonous). I started playing with it in the water and then was laughing and giggling—like a giggle that I hadn't giggled in a really long time since I was a little girl playing uninhibited and lost in her play.

All of a sudden I looked up and what I saw made my jaw drop and my eyes bulge in my goggles. A female dolphin was in the water facing me—so I turned to face her in my awe.

I asked her how she was. She said she was well and the next thing I know I started feeling a golden energy beaming through my stomach.

I asked her, "What are you doing?" and she said, "What do you think I'm doing?"

I said, "I don't know what you're doing but I do feel the golden energy that you are sending through my stomach," and she hung there and she giggled.

All I could remember due to the enormity of that moment (which felt like being suspended in time) was a feeling that something inside my stomach that had always felt nervous or stressed out or uncertain about myself and life and not totally confident had shifted itself. When that dolphin had connected with me on a level that I didn't even understand, I would later come to understand it as *Communion*.

After she giggled and realized that the energy she sent had sunk into my body and my being, she swam off. I was left standing there in the ocean with my snorkel and fins trying to somehow rationally comprehend what had just taken place.

It would take me many years of working with hundreds of animals to finally understand what she did in that moment for me. She had unlocked my tense stomach which was restricting my brain's ability to connect with the Quantum Energy Field that I had spent years before preparing for with my qigong practice...unwinding and cultivating my vital life force for this exact moment and this exact meeting.

In the moments after meeting this amazing creature in the ocean, I saw that the other dolphins in the bay were closer, so I swam out to be with them and my retreat friends. I felt like I had just been visited by the angels as the trumpets and bells sounded, and I realized that I could Commune-icate with the animals. I felt like this was the moment I was born for. Because in that moment I realized that my dream of helping sick animals heal was now going to become a reality by becoming an Animal Commune-icator™.

I became aware that Animal Communication would help me speak directly with the animals and hear them so that I could share with their humans exactly what they were feeling and needing straight from their mouths. There would be no guessing, no figuring out—just clear communication.

That day the healing channel that the dolphin opened in my brain helped me to understand a new level of Communion, not just with the white-haired and bearded old man who walks with a walking stick up in the sky, but as a way of living my life daily where I would realize more deeply that I am a part of All Life and All Life is a part of me.

Up until that point I had basically understood *Communion* only from what was spoken about in church, where one takes communion by putting a wafer in their mouth and drinks red wine to symbolize communion with Christ the God-consciousness.

That dolphin connected me with a new level of feminine communion with the wild ones that would end up unfolding for many years to come. I would move in a whole new direction as an Animal Commune-icator, which has allowed me to fulfill my childhood dream of helping sick animals heal.

WHAT IS THIS NEW COMMUNION?

I would learn from the Divine Feminine aspect of energy that there is a state of oneness that all life is capable of experiencing and that all life actually lives in. The number-one thing that takes us out of that is actually the number-one thing that humans pride themselves on: the intellect. Our intellect of logic and reason literally cut us off from dropping into the center of communion that takes place in the physical body and also on a quantum cellular level.

My experience of *Communion* feels like a state in which I am so connected to another being, I almost don't know where they end and I begin. It's not codependence, as dependencies are very different type of a connection that have an energetic hook embedded into it. *Communion*, however, is completely free and a sovereign experience.

This is the way the Native and Tribal peoples have always lived—in a deep connection with mama Gaia and with all the animals, plants, trees... with all life. This communion is about being asked to reclaim your soul so you can be at one with all life.

This communion is something that every mammal on the planet, every tree, every rock, every drop of water, every molecule of air knows and understands as *the* way of life. The only ones who have forgotten this are humans.

I started to truly understand this after working with thousands and thousands of animals remotely—animals that I didn't even touch in person as they were two thousand miles away! Yet here I was, able to help them heal their health and behavior issues without laying a hand on them.

This understanding of helping animals heal was beyond the science and math I had learned in school, beyond the science and math of quantum physics and quantum reality, and beyond the quantum energy field. I realized this was the truth of our cells being in Communion. I believe this is what is being explained as "mirror neurons" and quantum entanglements in science.

This became my zone of genius because animals would trust me and allow me to do things for them naturally. There was no surgery or pills, simply the natural energy of Communion.

I have been living in this state for quite a long time now. I admit that I have a harder time with humans than with animals, but when I can get the humans to drop into this quantum field of communion, everything flows with such ease and grace. And, this state of communion is based in modern physics which I *never in a million years* thought I would ever understand.

This is the highest level at which the earth operates, and it is now that we are coming to understand on an intellectual level this new level of communion. It's not about having to give over your body to anyone, rather it's about getting back into your body and being at one with everything—including the animals and the plants and the rocks—and understanding your part in the completely interconnected Web of Life.

So now I set sail on a new journey...

...a journey to teach others the art of communion with the animals, so that as humans we may understand on the deepest levels what this experience is. This is an opportunity to let our gut instincts inform our intellect and bring us into a state of oneness with All Life.

Allecia Evans is lovingly called The Animal Heeler™. If Dr. Doolittle, Gabby Bernstein, Albert Einstein, and Iyanla Vanzant had a love-child it would be Allecia. She is a unique combination of Professional Animal Commune-icator™, Holistic Dog Trainer, Medical Intuitive, Quantum Energy Field Bodyworker, and Soul Relationship Coach.

For over 24 years she has been a translator for the animals providing precise, accurate, and often lifesaving information to thousands of humans about their animal's health, behavior, soul partnership, natural leadership, natural nutrition, and crossing over issues, providing healing on both ends of the leash and reigns.

As the creatrix of **www.thewhitewolfway.com**, Allecia offers direct energy transmissions from the Wild Female Matriarchs to share their ancient wisdom with modern-day female and male leaders. She brings leaders on retreat with the Wild Ones to reconnect with and reclaim their transparent instinctual leadership essence.

A highly regarded expert on Dog Bio-Mechanics, Allecia has assisted 19,000 humans in teaching their dogs to HEEL safely and respectfully by inventing "The Walk In Sync™ Humane Dog Walking and Training System". She is the author of *The In Sync Method of Dog Training™: 6 Secrets Your Dog Wants To Teach You To Unleash Your Greatest Potential* and *The Missing Link In Dog Training: What Your Dogs Body Will Tell You About Their Behavior.*

Her ground-breaking distance energy healing work was the inspiration for and is featured in the book, *Soul Dog: The Spiritual Lives of Animals* as well as the documentary, "Listening To The Horse".

She is an award-winning TV host, radio show host, and columnist. Her work has been featured in, Aspen Magazine, The New Your Daily News, The Aspen Times, Animal Wellness Magazine, Listening To The Horse, and Dogtipper.com, as well as on Fox and Friends, The Sandra Glosser Show, and Aspen 82. Learn more at **www.thewhitewolfway.com.**

Special Gift

WILD MATRIARCH MEDITATION

Join Allecia in this exquisite 18-minute guided meditation that will reconnect you deeply and directly with the heart of the Wild Matriarchs. Allow yourself to experience your most natural state of Communion as you dissolve our human imposed separation from the Wild Matriarchs.

Access here: **https://db.tt/J0d2eQigYZ**

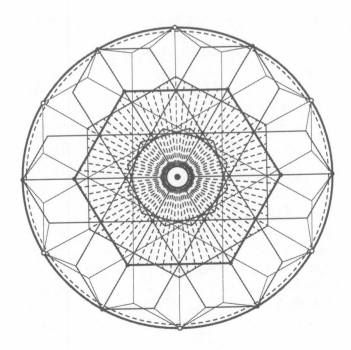

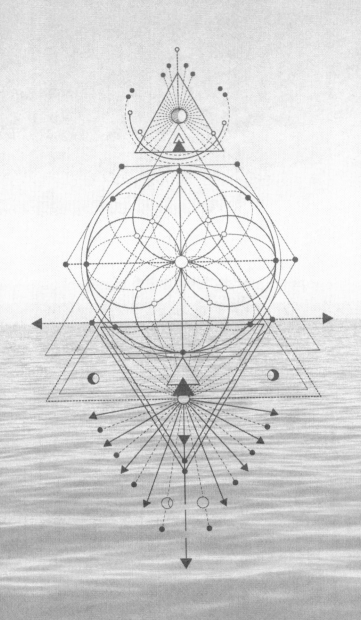

10 Ways to Cultivate Resilience, So You Can Flow with Change

BY JULIANNE JOY

There is only one constant in life...and that is change. I know that I am meant to embrace and flow with change, and although I am in a place of surrender now more than ever before, I still continue to struggle with it. Change is cyclical and includes deep processes such as life, death, and rebirth. Everything on earth has a life cycle, including humans, animals, nature with her four seasons, and the moon with her eight phases—from new moon to the full moon and all of the phases in between.

Adjusting to change is a spiritual path. We can't stay stagnant or our life force energy gets dimmed, and we cannot shine and share our gifts with the world in this condition. It takes courage to change your life. Raw, bold, loving courage.

I am learning how to flow with more ease and grace during times of change and, as a result, have built up my resilience. Resilience can be cultivated by checking your thought patterns, taking back your power, evaluating your attachment to control, prioritizing self-care, and being present in each moment.

One must be like a warrior and stand strong in the face of life's challenges. Here are 10 steps that will help you cultivate resilience and build the skills necessary to be in alignment in body, mind, and spirit:

1. CHECK YOUR THOUGHT PATTERNS

When we become aware of our thoughts and beliefs, we can then begin the process of change. Truthfully, letting go of old habits, patterns, and limiting beliefs has never been easy or comfortable for me. Letting go seems like such a simple solution, right? But it can be difficult to overcome the fear of the unknown about what's on the other side of change. The process of letting go begs one to ask, "If not this...then what? If not now...then when?" As humans, we always want to know what will happen next because we crave the comfort, safety, security, and predictability of knowing what we need to deal with.

Unconscious patterns and limiting beliefs keep us in a mindset prison. You may not even be aware of these patterns that happen in the unconscious software of your subconscious, because it doesn't happen in your thinking mind. But these patterns create loops that keep us stuck in fear. The time is here to release these old beliefs and patterns that don't serve us.

2. TAKE BACK YOUR POWER

Over the years, many energetic hooks have kept me playing small and not blossoming into my fullest potential. Family, pets, relationships, belongings, homes, even my clutter...these energetic hooks have all acted as distractions that have kept me from taking action. I have also found myself woven into a tangled web of relationship dynamics with others. These entanglements have kept me safe because they are familiar, but also have kept me stuck and painfully aware of how my life lacks the vitality and adventure I truly desire. I have learned that trying to please everyone around me is self-betrayal, and in relationships, I take back my power by being true to myself and by standing steadfast with my boundaries. You can do this, too, and reclaim your right to a happy life.

3. EVALUATE YOUR ATTACHMENT TO CONTROL

Our relationships are like mirrors, projecting back what is actually going on inside of us. We can use each other as mirrors so that we can learn and grow. In my case, I have been strangled by controlling personalities in my life, and then questioned, "Is it me who is actually the one who is controlling?"

I finally realized that I needed to set boundaries in my relationships to protect my own energy. Stronger boundaries will help you to trust your own inner authority, take better care of yourself, and not allow other people to define you. Boundaries also contribute to your emotional well-being, confidence, and self-worth.

Sometimes it seems so much easier to just stay where we are and not grow! Because then, there's no need to learn new things or adjust to change. But that also means that no one, including the planet, will benefit from your gifts. And if you are reading this book, I have a feeling you are here to serve and lead on a grander scale.

4. PRIORITIZE SELF-CARE

When you decide to take care of yourself first, you are teaching others how to treat you as well. Self-care is not selfish. We must take care of ourselves first in order to have the energy to take care of others.

Forgiveness is an act of self-care. Forgiving others is a tool to help *you* release any lingering negativity, regardless of what they end up doing. When we don't forgive others and instead hold grudges, it's like drinking poison and expecting the other person to die. The only one being hurt by my negativity is *me*. Dare to live fully by practicing self-care, as this is vital to your well-being.

5. GET PRESENT, CONNECT WITH YOUR INNER KNOWING, AND OWN YOUR POWER!

Being quiet and still can help us connect with our intuition...our inner knowing...our truth! When we trust our intuition, we can show up as our real selves, without any "masks" or barriers to our truth. Being seen for who we really are builds confidence and self-worth. One of the ways I connect to my inner knowing is through meditation. With practice, meditation will free you from the narratives that were imposed upon you, not chosen by you, such as, "I'm not good enough." That's powerful! Meditation will ignite your fire and unleash your true spirit so you can be the person you were meant to be.

I recently experienced Davidji's "RPM" meditation routine. It stands for "Rise, Pee, and Meditate." Basically, it means don't do anything else in between. Get right to your meditation pillow as soon as you go to the bathroom (since you won't be able to focus otherwise) and don't get distracted doing something else in between. This is key because when you first wake up, you are closest to your sleeping state, which is when your subconscious mind is most active and creative. This is the part of your mind that is not fully aware but influences your actions and feelings.

I found that when I tried Davidji's method, I connected to my center almost immediately and had chills all over my body. I felt an alignment in my body like *never* before. Pure bliss! As I was meditating, a sense of oneness came over me and I knew deep in my soul that *we are all one*—that *anything* we do affects one another. It all goes back to the circle of life—what goes around comes around.

We must be kind and compassionate if we want to receive that in return, because that is what we will attract back to us. We are all simply energy, and vibration attracts like vibrations. This is why we can attract abundance when we raise our vibration to that frequency, just like a radio antenna attracts a certain radio station frequency.

6. UNHOOK FROM DISTRACTIONS AND FEARS

When you focus on your values instead of your fears, you can then begin to unhook from distractions and energetic hooks and instead embrace liberation and sovereignty. In this way, you can stay present, rather than staying stuck in your past and in your old stories. Finding peace is an inside job; no one can do this work for you. We are each solely responsible for ourselves. Only you can do your work. This may entail slowing down, getting quiet, and listening. When you are open to receiving, you will be guided by a force greater than yourself. You can either continue to do the same things day after day and not change a thing or decide to pay attention and wake up to a better and more peaceful way of living. You have the power of choice and can choose to create a lifestyle that supports who you really are and what you value.

7. THE MAGIC OF RELEASING AND DECLUTTERING

When it's time to set sail off into a new direction in your life, all the hooks and the status quo must be released, so you can instead take a quantum leap into trust to see what the Divine has in store for you. You must also release your attachment to material things and consuming. I recently released my tiny home by the water in Rhode Island. It is so bittersweet. I have had so many years of happiness there, but I knew deep in my soul that it was time. I am trusting that there will be something better on the other side, although I don't know what that is yet.

When you release things in your life, you create a vacuum for better things and opportunities to enter your life. You can create space for better things and opportunities to show up by removing what no longer serves you in your physical space—let go and surrender it to the Universe. Be attentive to the signs and synchronicities along your path. Take action when necessary. Notice your opportunities and stay in a positive state of mind. Understand that you will not know what lies ahead, so simply have a sense of wonder and play in your life like a child. Dance and move your body to ground yourself and stand in your power. Speak your truth to cross the bridge on your path and get to the other side where beauty and abundance live. Find out what the universe has in store for you.

After selling my tiny house in Rhode Island, I was able to relax and savor my lake house more. I no longer had the pull to be in multiple places at once, thinking I might be missing out on something good in one place or the other. So I was able to surrender and really enjoy the present moment of boating on the lake. It feels good to simplify my life and be more fulfilled with less.

8. DANCE LIKE NOBODY'S WATCHING

Have you ever noticed how your perception of something changes based on where you are in that particular period of your life? This morning I went to a Zumba workout class. I had done Zumba a few times before, but something was different this time. Wow! It was such a liberating experience to be able to shake my body (in a room of mostly women) to music that made my body come alive and my soul sing. And there was no shame! Everyone else in the room was doing the same...we were all moving, flowing, and freeing our bodies to the music. It was joyful *and* we were burning calories at the same time. It is so therapeutic to be able to dance and release old feelings from your body in this fun and exuberating way. It felt like such a safe environment to release old threads of shame and doubt as we moved to the rhythm of the music.

9. FLOW WITH THE SAILS

Recently, I spent a few hours at Watch Hill, Rhode Island. The water was such a beautiful blue, and the sailboats were floating gracefully, making me feel so calm and relaxed. A feeling of freedom swept over my body as I imagined sailing away on one of the boats. After walking along the grassy paths by the water, I visited one of my favorite upscale stores. I felt so abundant as I basked in the beauty of the colors, the touch of the fine linens, the smell of the salty air, and the luxurious feel of the warm sunshine on my body. Noticing and appreciating the beauty all around me is one of my strengths.

I took some pictures and shared them with friends so they could feel the beauty and abundance as well. Sharing abundance makes you even more abundant, and by noticing and appreciating beauty, you will attract more beauty to you. When I am in this state of mind, it is as if I am floating through life. Some people call it *flow state*. I notice that I can manifest more when I'm in a flow state and am able to easily spot the synchronicities all around me. One time, a girlfriend suggested that I "Be the Warrior, not the Worrier." I saw that same saying in a store shortly afterward. Synchronicities happen often when I am just Being.

Have you stepped into the life you really want? Or are you still living other people's lives by doing what *they* want you to do? By being present in your life and noticing what is important, you will align your life with your values. It will be easier for you to set boundaries in all areas of your life once you know what is important to *you*. Once you do this, you will know when to say *no* and when to say *hell, yes!* It's time to stop feeling guilty about saying no and hiding in shame about things that happened in the past. You can finally begin to trust your inner knowing and flow with the sails.

10. CHOOSE LOVE OVER FEAR

You have the power to guide your emotions and instantly manifest a new reality by choosing love over fear. There is so much conflict, fighting, and upheaval on the earth at this time, and fear disconnects us from our infinite potential. The only way to heal this disconnection is with *love*. It can be difficult for people to understand and be patient when something bad happens to them, but we must stop and listen before we respond. We may not know the whole story about why someone is reacting the way they are. We have to be able to see things from the other person's perspective and come from a place of unconditional love. Only then can we transmute negative feelings to positive feelings of love, compassion, and understanding. Humor is a fabulous tool for transmuting lower vibrations and is powerful medicine for the soul. When you can find the humor in a situation, it helps by lifting any tension you may be experiencing and elevating you instantly into joy. Did you know that joy is portable? You can bring it with you everywhere you go!

Enjoy the journey because It's time to dance and play—and start living! What are you waiting for? Abundance is everywhere, and there is more than enough for everyone. Abundance is not just money, it is beauty, nature, meaningful relationships, and connection. It is the luxurious sense of fullness of joy and strength for your mind, body, and soul. Being grateful for what you already have attracts more abundance to you.

Nature holds so much life, and I'm noticing the sacred geometry in everything I see. You, too, can relish in that beauty and truly enjoy feeling the joy and sense of vibrancy and vitality that comes from being in alignment with your life. And always remember that rejection is simply redirection to something better.

Every one of us has the ability to transmute feelings of fear and anger into feelings of love. So let's do it together—right here, right now:

Joy is your birthright!

Keep cultivating resilience in your life and you will find that joy is front and center in your awareness and life is filled with laughter, love, and endless gratitude!

Julianne Joy is a Certified Public Accountant (CPA) and partner at Simione Macca & Larrow LLP. Throughout her career of more than thirty years, she has built her practice based on the foundation of relationships and serves her clients with the ultimate goal of seeking to do what is best for each client. She graduated from the University of Connecticut with a Bachelor of  Science degree in Accounting and has provided accounting, auditing, consulting, and tax services to a wide variety of industries, including clients in architecture, engineering, construction, real estate, insurance, manufacturing, printing, and not-for-profit.

In addition to her work in accounting and auditing, Julie advocates for her clients by supporting them with tax planning and projections and guiding them through tax audit representation with the Internal Revenue Service and State of Connecticut. She has also assisted clients with financial reporting, accounting and cost controls, systems, business planning, mergers and acquisitions, financing, and cash flow analysis, playing a critical role by acting as a catalyst for her clients to navigate their businesses, especially through times of change.

Julie is certified in Reiki 1, is a certified Law of Attraction Basic Practitioner, and is a Numerology Academy certified practitioner. She is also a member of the American Institute of Certified Public Accountants and the Connecticut Society of Certified Public Accountants, where she served on several committees over the years including the Federal Tax, Community Service, and Continuing Education Committees. She served a three-year term as a member of the National PCPS Technical Issues Committee, which monitors technical issues and developments in accounting, auditing, professional ethics, peer review, and governmental accounting that could have significant effect on closely held companies, not-for-profit organizations, government, and the CPAs who service them. She also served on the Professional Issues Task Force. Julie enjoys collaborating and networking with the expanding world marketplace through MSI Global Alliance, an international network of more than 250 legal and accounting firm connections in more than 100 countries.

A founding member of Women's Wellness Fund at Middlesex Hospital, Julie is actively involved in the Women's Business Alliance of Middlesex Chamber. She enjoys giving back to the community by being actively involved in causes close to her heart through volunteer opportunities that support animals, the environment, and healthcare. Most of all, Julie enjoys spending time with her family and Chinese crested dog, Isadora. Learn more at **www.juliannejoy.me.**

Special Gift

FREE GUIDED AUDIO MEDITATION

Only have a few minutes for self-care? If so, you'll love this short and relaxing guided meditation from Julianne Joy. You'll balance your chakras and get grounded so you can set focused daily intentions and create what you want in your life.

Access here: **www.Juliannejoy.me/setsailmeditation**

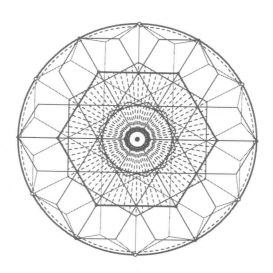

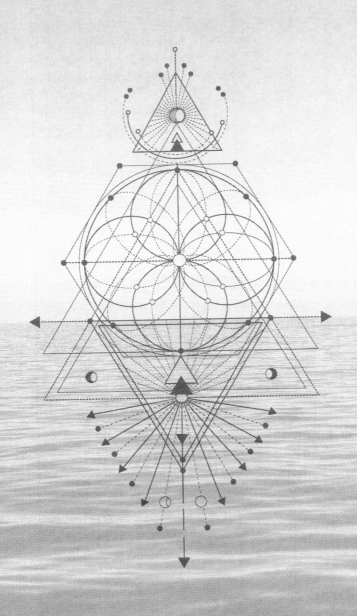

Into the Eyes of the Sacred: Reclaiming the Dark Moon

BY SHARDAI KLUGER

As you receive the words of this medicine story, drinking its
nectar deep into your belly, it activates and awakens an ancient
remembrance, meant just for you.
Sip slowly and mindfully...

I clutch the rotted old piece of bark I had intuitively picked up on my way to attend the death fire ceremony. "What is it that is ready to die within me? What is my offering to the fire?" I ponder the prompt our Vision Quest guides had given us. I hadn't known what to bring to the ceremony until this moment. Sometimes you don't have the foresight to prepare for the moment of transformation until it is upon you, beckoning you forward into the dark night. I sit on the red-dirt ground, flanked by a grove of aspens, and encircled by a grove of twenty other adults asking themselves the same questions.

I turn the bark over in my hands, caressing its wrinkled skin and knotted knuckles—listening for its medicine. "What did my body know by picking it up? What needed to die so that my life could continue?" Surely it was something, or else it wouldn't have drawn me miles away into the desert—and deep into my vulnerability—with a group of strangers willing to relinquish four days of food and companionship to set their lives straight again.

I start to shiver uncontrollably from the dry night air piercing through my woolen layers, and from the chattering of the ancient ones making noise from within. I listen deeply to the shares of those brave enough to go before me. And I peer longingly into the flames at the center of our circle, as they lick and consume the sacrificial wooden logs. For a moment I get swept into the dance of the warm light as it sparks upward against the cool darkness, mirrored by the crystalline stars. This dance—encapsulating the wild tale of my becoming.

My heart starts to race, and I suddenly know what is coming. The fire shifts, sending a branched finger pointing directly at me.

My turn.

I have always been fascinated by ceremony. My siblings and I played 'church' often, when we were younger. We would roll up Wonder bread into doughy balls, then squish it into flat spheres underneath our tiny palms and offer it to each other as Holy Sacrament. Dressing up in our oversized 'Sunday best' straight from our parents' closet, and gathering the finest table clothes and silver platters, we dramatized the whole service as we knew it— beginning to end. It was ever-magical, and quite a source of amusement for my parents, I'm sure.

I became a full-on Bible-thumper after my first ecstatic tango with the Divine. Hands raised, speaking in tongues, coming up crying onto the altar... this was real. This was profound. I could feel it in every cell of my ripening twelve-year-old body. Yet as much as I tried, I couldn't quite express it to anyone in the same form that I had received it in. My direct experience of the Divine was somehow lost in the packaging process of Christianity. And my evangelistic attempts to share it, fell flat.

I became bitter at those who didn't have the heart to acknowledge that there was something here to be listened to. Something of great importance. An importance that I couldn't then explain, yet there it was, peering back at me through the holes in the very rhetoric I was attempting to explain it through.

It is a gaze that has haunted me ever since.

Father, Son, Holy Ghost, Priest, Bishop, Pope...Men 'granting' me access to the Divine everywhere I looked. On the church altar, the priorities were clearly displayed: Jesus at the center, and women on the flanks. I felt an authentic respect for, and connection to the path Jesus walked, yet behind that star-lined veil of Mother Mary, I could see an even deeper truth awaiting me. What wisdom was concealed within this most delicate and alluring fabric? What secrets did she have to tell?

And where had all the women gone?

As I excuse myself from class, I hold a wadded-up bundle of Kleenex, with a discreetly wrapped tampon inside of my palm, praying the High School boys and chatty girls would be none-the-wiser. It is from a stash of 'sanitary goods' that my mom had quietly placed in my room at the first signs of my emerging pubescence. She always made everything into something special, much to my solitary-seeking teenage dismay. It had taken me a couple of weeks to summon the courage to tell her about starting my period. After a tensely silent car ride to my dance practice one evening, I finally forced the words out in some nonchalant fashion. For some reason this was an intimate fact that I felt would let her into my world a little too closely. And it felt like my own dirty secret to keep.

I make my way into the stall, conscious of not taking too long, so as to not draw suspecting attention. My girlfriends and I had an agreement that we would check each other for leaks through our jeans and report them if necessary. This rarely happened, but it was a comfort to have some reprieve from the constant ponderings of the worst-case humiliation stories.

On these first few days of my cycle, I would grind through my classes, trying to hide the fact from those around me that I was in severe pain. It was a pain I would rather die from instead of embrace. And I had no choice but to push my body onward. Track. Dance. Choir. Honors Classes. There was no way I could stay ahead of my learned expectations of excellence, while excusing myself from several days of school each month. This was a normal part of being a woman now, and I just needed to accept it.

I spent years in the allopathic medicine circuit. First as a nurse's aide to pay my way through nursing school, then as a hospital nurse. My body knew its trappings years before my brain did. When I was in my junior year of nursing school I fell ill overnight. I awoke with an insanely painful migraine and the ongoing desire to vomit—though I never was granted such relief.

I spent the next few months in and out of the ER where I worked. I waited miserably for hours in the non-life-threatening queue, underwent some tests, received no answers, vomited up pain meds, went back to classes, and then back to the ER. Each month when I was menstruating my experience of this amplified. I passed six kidney stones from dehydration, and my body became scarily malnourished from not being able to keep down more than soda crackers and ginger ale. As time went on, I became deeply depressed, and so shut down on every level of my being—I could barely muster a response to my free work therapist, as she grilled me for a grueling hour each week. I was clamped down like a steel trap around a broken and bleeding leg.

I let myself bleed-out like this for months within the walls of my dormitory, in silence.

Unseen. Unimportant. Unfixable.

Death would be better than this.

I spent all summer paying off my medical bills through my nursing internship in cardiac rehab. Sensing that I was the one who really needed this rehab of the heart—wounded from the institutions of education and health that were requiring me to pay them back their own debts. I started to question what I was learning. Where were all these answers I was assured by 'the experts' in healthcare?

Where had all the healers gone?

After encountering the same disillusionment of education in Chinese Medicine School—and as an ode to the teenage rebellion I never gave myself permission to express—I dropped out, sold all my things, bought an old vintage 1970s RV, and made my way up the California coast to join an alternative education program: Weaving Earth.

I spent the first ten days crying.

I simply could not help it; something was opening up in me that had been unacknowledged for so long and was literally crying to be heard and released. I had hit the infamous wall of grief. The wall that I now know stands between what someone thinks they are, and who they truly are.

As my worldview opened up slowly, I began the arduous journey of confronting my life. Over the next three years, I slowly unlearned much of what I'd been taught about the world and relearned my authentic connection to it. It was treacherous beauty. I was stretched, challenged, confronted, and disassembled from the inside out. I learned the plants not from a pouch as in Chinese Medicine School, but from asking them about their medicine gifts as they grew there in front of me. I slept under the stars and harmonized with my sisters around the fire late into the night. I tracked animals through the moss-covered oaky woods and found my throne upon the forest stones.

I felt alive again.

I joined in on the conversation nature was having all around me, and on every possible level—I started to listen.

And to speak.

At our Women's Moon Lodge at Weaving Earth—our dedicated space for women on their Moon Time, or menstruation time—I would be tended to, and other times tend after other women in our community. It was here, during our bleeding times, where we sisters relearned how to part the veils of the mystery and peer into the eyes of the Sacred. If you paid attention, you could, in turn, encounter the Sacred through the shimmering eyes of these bleeding women. The face of the Divine lingers upon us like this during ceremony, a mirror for all to see.

This Moon Woman's body would learn to pour forth its offering each darkened moon, with the ecstatic labor of giving birth reeling her into an altered state of consciousness. It was from that state, where she could drink the sweet nectar of the Goddess deep into her belly. She would then offer it to the Earth with her prayers, and its wisdom to her community. She was a conduit, completing the energetic cycle between Cosmos and Earth. She was the Divine *mattering*.

One day I was called to come tend to a sister who was experiencing the piercing pain that would come with this time of the month for her. I could relate.

Somehow we both knew I could help.

I intuitively placed my hands on her lower back, as she curled forward into child's pose, and pressed her face into the soft red rug. Amidst the billowing of the canvas tent against the unrelenting wind, and the groans and pants of this bloody birthing, I dropped into a peaceful presence with her. With eyes closed, I began to gently knead her lower back as if I was preparing an earthen clay vessel. My hands, gently pushing through the soil of her flesh, excavating and re-molding this uterus, into something that could be of use to her again—a vessel of the Divine. Through the piercing eyes of my inner sight, I followed the desires of her body-softening, turning, creating more space, more permission, more alignment. Providing a safe space for her womb to occupy again: "It's okay, nothing will harm you now, you are home." Her whole body gave a deep and cathartic exhale, and the pain was forever released into the past.

My hands were channels for the Divine Mother to enter her. My presence the soothing balm. Together, we had courted the Ancient Woman that lived inside of her. It was as if She was waiting for us to *see* Her, bring Her roses, feed Her chocolates and anoint Her feet with Sacred oils... When my sister chose to listen to Her voice within her body, how easily She responded—with the loving arms of a mother who was greeting her child back home.

This was healing.

This was the Divine.

Panic. Impending doom.

I am going to die. I have no idea why or how, but I feel it shaking through every cell in my body.

My car barely grips the edges of the turns along the California Highway 1, as I make an emergency trip to Phyllis's healing space. She is a traditional Mexican Curandera I had happened upon and began to train with during my days off from Weaving Earth.

I was scared of her at first. Unsure of whether or not I was safe with this dark, Bear-like old woman and her seemingly altered sense of reality. Having learned to fear darkness as evil my whole life, I was unsure of how to trust this woman who was comfortable with and seemed to attract it. Yet here I was, being drug down by the demons and voices of my childhood nightmares, and this woman of mystery was there to guide me through it.

Greeting me with her thick hands, and knowing gaze, she invites me to the floor and wraps me in her Buffalo hide rug. My panic slowly melts into the ground as she smokes her medicine pipe—her vessel of communication with my ancestors—as I drift off through the layers of my subconscious, and into the underworld...

It seems there is no end to the screaming that I hear from within me. I started to hear it when I was a small child. In an attempt to explain it to my parents I said I was 'hearing voices,' yet I had a strange knowing that these dark chatterings were created from within *me* somewhere.

I didn't yet understand that my ancestors had chosen me. That they were speaking to and through me. That they needed to support me to do my spiritual work, so I could help them to do theirs. Phyllis was helping me see that the illness that overtook me during nursing school was my soul crying out to be seen. My ancestors responded to these cries by helping me to purge the binding structures of the human world that were keeping me small and useless to my greater purpose. Each Moon Time, they were signaling through the messenger hormones of my body, this remembrance of who I truly was. And like a tree sending its roots down into the earth to seek nourishment, they were slowly piercing and cracking through the thickened soil of my head, my heart, and my womb, so I may be able to more fully receive the sustenance my soul was craving.

And here again, my ancestors are back, whispering into my ear: "It's time to do more work." They have already stepped across the threshold into death, and so in a way, they are the perfect ones to usher me through this next spiritual death...

Jennifer Berezen's voice drones on through Phyllis's old CD player, as I give myself over more fully to the healing journey...

"Returning...

Returning...

Returning...to the Mother of us all..."

I remember the feeling of stepping into my first ceremonial lodge, set years later by my shamanic Maestro, don Oscar Miro-Quesada. All of my senses were immediately overtaken. The feeling of expansive love, intentionality, and pure presence, sharing space with the power of all the unseen beings there ready to support us on our humble Earth-walk. The air thickened with the tangible substance of Life. The glimmering medicine altars in front of every person, so unique to their expression of the Divine, imbued with arti-facts that have given their lives meaning. The sounds of bells and rattles, and the flicks of feathers. The billowing smoke from burning incense, filling my nostrils, dissolving and shape-shifting the images of everyone in the room.

How right it felt to take my seat there.

"It's all smoke and mirrors," Maestro likes to say. Life and everyone in it, is this grand projection screen upon which we visualize who We are, who We once were, and who We are becoming. And it is our task to see beyond the billowing illusions, into the truth of our essence. To offer our-selves up to life as a sacrifice—in the true meaning of the word—to make ourselves Sacred.

The repetition of ritual tradition has cleared a pathway for the Divine to arrive here easily, just as it did in my childhood church. The Divine surfaces through the cross I now keep at the center of my medicine altar, a crossroads that for me, marks the intersection of the Divine Masculine *and* the Divine Feminine. All that has been, and all that will be. All that is Holy, and all that is Profane.

During one of our medicine lodges, my Maestro don Oscar tells us the story of a ceremony he had orchestrated at a national conference of esteemed Indigenous Elders. As I understand it, he bravely offered it in order to bring his Peruvian culture's perspectives to the political power structures that were still unconsciously keeping the Feminine suppressed.

The ceremony ensues as a stone 'mountain' or apacheta, is built outside as the central altar. It is an energetic linking of the Cosmos and the Earth, and a receptacle for offerings and prayers. The participating women come into the center; with vessels of moon-blood they had collected from women around the nation, and pour the contents forth onto the stones at the center. When they are complete, the power of the black puma is let loose, so to speak, and the magic of the ceremony climaxes with such potency, that by the end, all of the Elders declare that Moon Women will be welcomed back into their tribal ceremonies again.

There is something about the symbology of this that strikes me to the core. *The moon blood was brought by the hands of the women, back into the center of ceremony again.* The power of that wild, magical, life-giving feminine was remembered by the men in that circle. It was respected again. *This is what needs to happen.* This magical nectar of the Sacred Feminine, once kept on the mysterious outskirts of the village, needs to be brought forward into the center, and remembered by all of us.

I am visibly stirred after receiving this story. My spiritual sisters gather around me, creating Sacred Space in which they witness and support me as my inner phoenix rises to meet my soul's calling. One sister stroking my hair and singing a medicine song flowing straight through from Spirit, and meant only for that moment in time. Another gently coaching me as she sees the imagery of what is transpiring with her gift of sight. A sister handfeeding me the sacrament of the most lusciously sensual strawberries I have ever tasted. And another, at my feet, anointing them with her loving touch. Tears slowly slide down my cheeks and bless the Earth below with my gratitude.

The Ancient Woman from within me had been re-membered at last, at the encouraging hands of these beautiful women.

"Welcome to Sisterhood."

The branched finger of the fire is pointing directly at me, beckoning me forth into the dark desert night.

My turn.

What is it that finally needs to be laid down to rest within me?

I spread a small amount of my own sacrosanct Moon Blood onto my wooden bark offering, and carefully make my way to the middle of our Vision Quest circle. The chattering of the ancient ones within my bones is getting louder. The fire swells and sparks with vengeance into the night sky. Visibly shaking now, as the grief and anger of millennia of murdered medicine women ripples through my flesh—ready to wail and scream out to the cool night sky, in horror!! I instead slowly kneel down onto my seat at the center, and simply sit still in empty presence.

As tears roll down my cheeks, and a great peace washes over me, I allow myself to speak silently to these ancestors through the fire. I see visions of the beautiful medicine women—the wisdom-keepers of the sacred—transforming into ashes by the flames of persecution sweeping the lands. At the hands of greedy men, yes, but perhaps also at the hands of our destiny to forget ourselves in order to re-member in a different way some day. I look down at the piece of once-mysterious bark, selected in a moment of knowing, and anointed both by the holiest elixir of life's potential, and by the grief of all that has been lost.

I hesitate before I offer it to the ritual fire...

This one small act is the telling of a very long and ancient story. It is mine and it is yours. It's a story that has taken me to the underworld and back again. It's the story of retrieving my Soul from the dark and mysterious womb of the Feminine. It is Forgiveness. Forgiveness of the essential self that has been crucified, and those that have crucified it. It is about reclaiming the primal fires of the Sacred Feminine that have been turned against Her—that are forced into the manicured barrels of guns and used as tools of warfare. This is a story of resurrecting life from the blood that is shed.

It is a story of embracing the Dark Moon in all of us; the chaos, the rage, the wild self, the sexual nature of life, the magic of the unexplainable—the unreal, and all that is misunderstood and thusly feared.

The darkness is now my purpose, my moon-blood my prayer, the underworld my ally, and this unpredictable and once-feared Medicine Woman—is now me.

I am ready to speak my prayer.

"May the Feminine never be harmed by fire again."

The coyote howls begin to pierce through the quiet desert air in agreement. The hauntings of the wild past reclaiming their voices again.

"We're still here. We're with you."

Standing tall now, with the night's reflection of true power in my eyes, I pitch my piece of decaying wood into the eternal flames of alchemy.

"This one's for the Witches."

Shardai Kluger, RN is a Priestess Initiate and Temple Guide, a Shamanic Teacher and Ceremonialist, a certified Reiki Master and Shamanic Energy Healer, and the Founder of Sacred Center Sanctuary: Center of the Sacred Arts.

She is a passionate beauty-guide, cosmic dreamer and lover of the wild, and deeply sourced from the roots of soul. She has dedicated her life in service to the healing of the Sacred Feminine and Masculine and to the reawakening of the Ancient One within us all. As a Sacred Enchantress, it is her life decree to be a voice and vessel of service to the Divine.

Shardai has a Western background as an RN, working in Adolescent Psychiatry, Pediatrics, Geriatrics, and Medical/Surgical Medicine, as well as with Western Herbalism and essential oils. She has an Eastern background in Chinese Medicine, Reiki, Yoga, and Insight Meditation. She also has an Earth-based background in Deep Nature Connection Mentoring, Cross-Cultural Shamanism, and Modern-Day Priestessing.

Through Sacred Center Sanctuary, she offers private healing sessions, mystery school initiations, shamanic apprenticeships, and community ceremony and ritual. In all her work, she uses the gifts of her hands as channels of the Divine, her heart as a field of compassionate love, her voice as a calling of soul, and her inner sight as an authentic mirror of your truth.

She currently resides with her sweetheart Naga, in Manitou Springs, CO, where she spends her free time wandering in the mountains, writing, sipping tea on the porch, making sometimes-funny witty remarks, and living synchronicities.

Shardai believes that the very wisdom and healing we seek, is seeking to be remembered from within us. It is her honor to help re-member You.

Learn more at **www.sacredcentersanctuary.com; facebook.com/ sacredcentersanctuary; IG: @sacred_center_sanctuary.**

Special Gift

GUIDED JOURNEY: INTO THE EYES OF THE SACRED

Join Shardai on a magical journey through space and time, cosmos and earth, to reunite with your Inner Ancient One. Be nourished by the vibrations of gem-infused crystal bowls and enchanted vocals. Part the veils between the worlds, and peer into the eyes of the Sacred...hear the call of your Inner Ancient One as She guides you through the fires of your inner knowing and delivers you to the clarity you are seeking at this time.

Getting to know and trust the voice of this One within you is an essential beginning step on the path of the Isis Mystery School Initiate—as taught by Sacred Center Sanctuary. You can find out more about our Mystery School offerings on our website.

Access here: **www.sacredcentersanctuary.com/setsail**

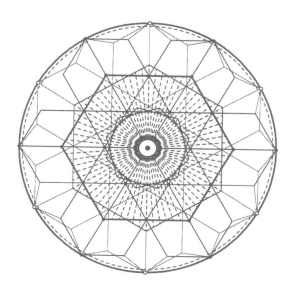

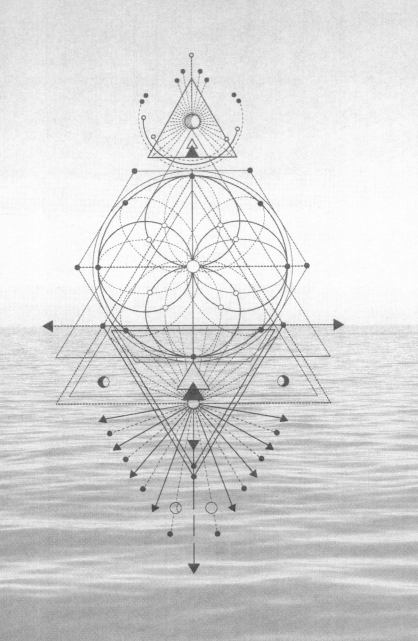

A Leap of Faith into Legacy

BY KARINA MOUNTAIN BLUEBIRD

Life, mysterious life
We're moving around dancing the rhythm of life
Time mysterious time
We're counting the hours and days to the end of time
We are feeling a change and don't know why
Choose one direction just one for a time
Don't say I'm thinking too much if you see what's behind
And these are the mysterious times
Mysterious times
No trick of the mind
For this moment I feel like we live in mysterious times
If you see what's behind
These are the mysterious times
Soul, I feel my soul
For this moment nobody can stop me from flying so high
Real, nothing is real in a world of illusion you only see what
you feel
We are feeling a change and we don't know why
Choose one direction just one for a time
Don't say I'm thinking too much if you see what's behind
And these are the mysterious times

—Sash!, lyrics from "Mysterious Times"

Our legacies, I believe, are preordained by our own orchestration, prior to coming into each lifetime. In that light of understanding, I chose my birth family's paradigm of growing up amongst five brothers. This defined my character, and this gave me the perspective I needed to make a difference in other women's lives. This is where I took my first steps as a young girl, learning to walk alone.

This experience and many others will be shared in my forthcoming book. These occurrences have defined my path as the archetypal energy of the "woman who walks alone." She is a modern-day archetype who has only been allowed the freedom to speak her truth during the past century. It has not been safe for her to be seen or heard since the early Egyptian and Greek eras of the Goddess, after the patriarchal leaders annihilated her. These Goddess energies are finally returning to us on Earth, although she has been calling us to embrace her for eons! Women are at last waking up everywhere on our planet.

My plan to drive to Mount Shasta for the Galactic Synchronization occurring on the winter solstice 2012 was completely derailed when I came across an advertisement for a yoga retreat in Tulum, Mexico. The Galactic Synchronization was the end of the Mayan calendar, beginning almost 26,000 years ago. This event was of great spiritual significance and people were gathering all over the world to acknowledge and honor it. The early Mayans believed it would be the end of the world.

Time,

mysterious time

Where we're counting the hours and days to the end of time...

—"Mysterious Times"

Taking the leap of faith, I flew to Cancun the following week and bused to Tulum and its white pearly beaches about 100 kilometers south. The fresh, salt air and calming ocean breezes reassured me that I made the right decision.

The ethereal realm of this spiritual mecca energized my body but challenged my logical mind. I was raised in a patriarchal Catholic family in the middle of five brothers. My father, a scientist, believed everything had to be tried, tested, and proved. I had to quiet that voice in my head and focus on my own free thinking, which my mother had inspired.

Each day my angel guides gave me a physical gift that made no sense to my rational mind. The first day a flat turquoise stone, two inches in diameter and in the shape of a buffalo, mysteriously appeared on the toe of my shoe as I was waiting at the airport.

Once in Mexico, on the second day I found what appeared to be an ancient handmade gold-and-copper braided ring under a rock outside the ruins of Tulum.

On the third day I had an encounter with a woman at the Coba ruins that further challenged my grasp of reality. I actually saw an insect metamorphose into a butterfly right between my forefinger and thumb as I went to pluck it from her shirt.

On the fourth day, the winter solstice, I was invited to a ceremony for locals by a healer I met at the yoga center in Tulum. This manifested into an occurrence that transported me into a past lifetime with the ancient Mayans.

None of this made any sense to my linear mind. I had been on a spiritual path for almost three decades, always searching for a deeper meaning to my existence. I have read many books about altered realities, parallel dimensions, and past lifetimes. But I had never experienced anything at this level of cognizance.

During a psychic reading the next day I was told there was a "lady of the lake" who was calling me to come assist in the healing of all nations. I had no idea what that meant or what I was supposed to do, but I recalled a prophecy that had been foretold to me by my spiritual teacher fifteen years earlier: "The White Buffalo Calf Woman will call upon you to bring forth her legend." At that time, I didn't even know who the White Buffalo Calf Woman was! As a reminder of my legacy, my teacher gifted me a spiritual relic decorated with beads and gemstones, complete with a hand painting of White Buffalo Calf Woman sitting on a buffalo holding a ceremonial pipe.

Soul,
I feel my soul
For this moment nobody can stop me from flying so high...

—"Mysterious Times"

The final evening of the Mayan calendar, I had a spiritual awakening during my meditation that was surreal yet incredibly lucid. I was standing before a council of nine elders, an androgynous group of high beings, who spoke to me telepathically, indicating it was my destiny in this lifetime to activate this ceremony and that I should go to Lake Titicaca, high in the Andes, without delay. The hair on my arm was standing straight up and there was a familiar prickling sensation under my skin that affirmed the validity of this strange occurrence for me. I had studied with South American shamans who trained me in performing ceremony, but I did not know what kind of ceremony I was supposed to perform for the White Buffalo Calf Woman or for what purpose.

I discovered that the legend of the White Buffalo Calf Woman dated back many generations, when she appeared to the Lakota-Sioux Indians bringing them the gift of the sacred pipe and teaching them how to use it for prayer and ceremony to heal their people from sickness and stop the famine they were enduring. As she walked away, she rolled on the ground four times, shapeshifting into a female buffalo calf, changing colors with each roll: from red representing the Native people, to black indicating the African people; to yellow symbolizing the Asian People; and finally white, signifying the Caucasians. Hence her name: White Buffalo Calf Woman. She promised that one day she would return to help bring unity and peace to earth.

The next morning, I canceled my return trip home and re-booked a flight to Peru. While I was waiting at the bus station to go to the Cancun airport, I tried to get some cash from the ATM. It kept my card and did not disburse any pesos! Upon arrival in Lima, I went to another ATM machine to get some Peruvian sols and to my mortification, that machine kept my credit card, too. I was now down to one credit card and still no cash. Yikes!

I was starting to worry that I had been misguided or that there were dark forces working against me. How could I have been given all these spiritual gifts of affirmation the week before that I was on the right path, and now I keep running into obstacles? Feeling nervous and sensing that something else unfortunate might happen next, I tottered to the gate to board my fight and fell fast asleep during the two-hour bumpy flight on the rickety old airplane. I was not sure if it would stay aloft, but I was too tired to care.

I was headed to Puno where I would catch a boat to an island on Lake Titicaca, where I was planning to meet my husband, Chuck. He and his daughter were hiking the Inca Trail to Machu Picchu during the Galactic Synchronization. We agreed to meet on the island of Amantani. The scenery was breathtaking, and the boat ride was exhilarating, however upon arrival,

I stared up with apprehension at the very steep zig-zag trail ascending the mountain. We were already at about 13,000-foot elevation and the village was about 14,000 feet. I was carrying a backpack that weighed thirty-five pounds, and I was not prepared for this level of exertion, so I agreed to pay a small sum to Armando, my guide, to carry my pack up the mountainside. He scurried up the trail as if he was a mountain goat while I steadied myself, taking each step carefully, inhaling long, slow, deep breaths. Armando gave me a bitter coca leaf to chew on to alleviate the nausea and lightheadedness.

When we reached the town plaza, Armando pointed in the direction where my husband waited. I looked over the stone wall and called out to him. He walked a few steps towards me and then suddenly collapsed over a rock. Both Armando and I ran down the hillside to see what had happened. We lifted his limp body from the rock. He mumbled he was weak and light-headed from the journey and needed some rest.

We retired that evening to a straw-filled mattress and windows with no screens or glass. The nighttime was amazingly quiet, with only the sound of Chuck's labored breathing. I could hear gurgling as if there was fluid in his lungs. The next morning, he was even weaker. Even though it was Christmas Day, I told the house owner that he needed a doctor. She instructed her son, Paulo, to get the village doctor. I was astonished that we could get someone on a pedestrian island to make a house call, especially on Christmas Day. She arrived within the hour, listened to his breathing with her stethoscope, and diagnosed him with edema. He paid the doctor a small fee, and she advised us to return to sea level as soon as possible, telling us that there was a clinic in Puno for people who were suffering from this condition. Edema is serious, possibly fatal if left untreated, and happens commonly to tourists who do not acclimatize to the high elevation.

That same day we left for Puno and Chuck spent the night in the clinic while I went to the Americana Hotel. The following morning a nurse walked around the village with us, while Chuck carried an oxygen tank on his back. All his vital symptoms were normal, so they released him. I rearranged our flights to leave two days later, both agreeing that I should go back to the island for the foreordained ceremony I had traveled so far to perform. He would stay in the room at the Americana and would be taken care of with room service and the oxygen they had already delivered to our room.

I rose at the crack of dawn and left for the port, knowing the first boat would leave at 7:00 a.m. and the last boat would depart from the island at

3:30 p.m. I took my passport, journal, some snacks, my ceremonial pipe and sacred tobacco, along with my only remaining credit card and $40 cash. I had noticed an ATM the last time we came into port, so before I purchased my boat ticket, I inserted my last credit card into the ATM while holding my breath and biting my lower lip. In disbelief, the ATM didn't disburse any cash and kept my last credit card! A wave of nausea overcame me, my knees went weak and I sank to the ground. Armando was at the port and saw this happen and came running to my aid. I blurted between my sobs of exasperation since I had last seen him only two days earlier. He offered to take me for free to the island of Taquile to the altar of Pacha-Mama and Pacha-Tata (Mother Earth and Father Sky). This sweet man was becoming my Earth angel!

At 9:00 a.m. I was still waiting on Armando's twenty-passenger ferry boat for their tour group to board. The tour stopped at a few of the reed islands, so my two-hour trip turned into a four-hour trip, and I needed to get to the shrine and be back to the dock no later than 3:30 p.m. to catch the last boat back to Puno.

During the boat ride, I was asking the Peruvian guide about the place I needed to get to, and I learned it was a poorly marked trail, identifiable only by markings of sticks and stones. I started having second thoughts about getting lost and losing time, so I asked Armando if he would be my guide and I could pay him the last $40 cash I had to bring me up and back. He graciously accepted, and as we disembarked the boat, he said he needed to stop by his home along the way to grab some provisions and his daypack. When we arrived at his very modest adobe home, he invited me in to meet his family. The floor was made of compressed dirt and in the corner of the open room was a pit of hot coals with a large pot perched on top of a rack. His daughter Juanita was making lunch in one pot and invited me to join them. I was already concerned about my time limitation and politely refused, but Armando insisted, saying he needed to eat before we went. I had no choice, if I wanted his assistance, so I accepted and ate my simple meal of stewed guinea pig and rice, taking each bite with a sense of trepidation overcoming me, knowing this was my last chance to fulfill my legacy.

Real,
nothing is real
in a world of illusion you only see what you feel...

—"Mysterious Times"

After lunch we hiked briskly, but it took us an hour, and at that point, I knew I would have to act quickly and run down the trail if I was going to catch the boat. I set up the ceremonial space on the worn stone altar and began the ceremony by calling in the four directions, something that I had learned from my studies with the South American shamans. I lit my ceremonial pipe, offered a prayer, and passed it with the mouthpiece facing towards Armando. in the ceremonial tradition. He took a deep long inhale from the sweet tobacco. We prayed for the healing of all nations and her peoples and then out of nowhere, the cloud-laden skies turned an ominous ebony that rumbled with thunder and shook the mountaintop.

Lightning crackled across the sky in a startling strike. And then the thunder rumbled and it began to pour. I yelled at the top of my lungs across the valley floor, "YO ESTOY AQUI; I AM HERE!", feeling like I finally accomplished my assigned mission. CRACKLE...BOOM!! There was a thunderous roar coming back at me as if to acknowledge my statement of fulfillment. The sky roiled with black clouds billowing overhead as I gazed up and saw the unmistakable image of a white buffalo appearing in the form of a white cloud in reverse contrast against the dark alto cumulus behind it. Overcome with joy, tears pooled in my eyes, as I dropped to my knees in honor and recognition of the White Buffalo Calf Woman. Armando was right beside me on his knees, as we bowed our heads in reverence. He looked sideways at me under his wide brimmed hat with a big grin, baring his decaying teeth, a residual from all the coca leaves he had chewed over his lifetime. We gathered our ceremonial artifacts quickly, and began to jog down the rocky, muddy trail as the rain pummeled our bodies. It took us about forty-five minutes to get down the mountain. We were soaked to the bone, but I was grateful that we both had hiking boots on that kept us from slipping and falling. As we careened the last corner coming through the village, I could see the boat pulling away from the dock. I screamed "No! Come back!" but my vain attempt at stopping it merely echoed across the turbulent waters.

And we're feeling the change and we don't know why.
Choose one direction just one for a time.
Don't say I'm thinking too much if you see what's behind...

—"Mysterious Times"

Through a series of trials and tribulations and mysterious synchronicities, I did make it back to Puno late that evening. I arrived back at my hotel dripping wet, only to discover that my husband had checked out of the room, taking my luggage with him and telling the front desk clerk he was going to the airport. I had no dry clothes, no cash, or no credit cards left. My story continues with the journey unfolding in my book being published in 2020, *Woman Who Walks Alone.*

Much has evolved on my spiritual path since this event took place seven years ago. I now know that my journey to Mexico and Lake Titicaca was pre-ordained in unperceived realms and reinforces my belief in the mysteries of the universe. One must be initiated into their own spiritual awakening and more often than not, the lessons are challenging, however crucial for the benefit of our own human evolution and spiritual growth. I am honored to have had this enlightening experience and I embrace the whole "SHE-Bang!"

This has been my self-realized legacy, following in the footsteps of the fearless women who walked alone before me. I am grateful to be in the "wise woman" era of my life. I am finally finding my own tribe of women who are walking the same path alongside me. "SHE" is forging a new path as we walk together, opening the way for the future of all women, together in service to each other and to humanity for the benefit of all mankind.

Karina Mountain Bluebird (Karen Petersen) was raised in rural upstate New York near the Adirondack mountains, which were first settled by the Mohawk Indians. She felt their presence in the heavily wooded land behind her family's home where she grew up and spent much of her adolescence playing with her pack of five brothers digging for Indian arrowheads and building forts. She intuitively resonated with the tribal ways of the Native Americans;  dancing with the elementals, discovering the ways of the warrior, and learning how to tap into nature's vibration through her deep connection to Mother Earth.

She was given her spiritual name "Karina Mountain Bluebird" in a ceremony on a reservation of the First Nations in Manitoba in northern Canada, while she was studying shamanism. There she went on a solo vision quest in search of her totem animal. Four periwinkle mountain bluebirds came to her, each one landing on the upper tipi posts where she could see them through the portal opening of the tipi to the sky. The posts in a tipi structure represent the trails from earth to the spirit world.

Karina leads Wild Woman retreats in the Rocky Mountains of Colorado. With her natural fire spirit, she is fiercely passionate about empowering women to forge their own path in the world. She has been initiated in the lineage of the 13 Moon Mystery School in Marin, California, founded by Ariel Spilsbury, where she commutes regularly between her wellness business on the San Francisco Bay and her sanctuary in the Rocky Mountains of Colorado.

Special Gift

20% DISCOUNT OFF YOUR FIRST
"WILD WOMAN" RETREAT OR WORKSHOP

Karina holds retreats to help women awaken into their archetypal
goddess energies. Please email her at **Shebewe@gmail.com**
if you would like to receive upcoming information about
workshops and retreats.

Mention this book and receive a 20% discount off your first
"Wild Woman" retreat or workshop.

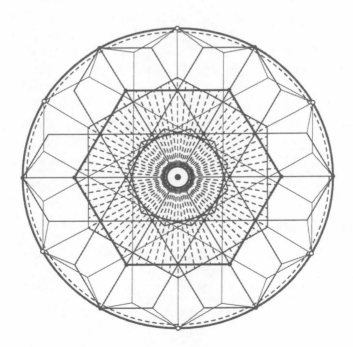

Unleash Your Wild Wisdom: Live Your Life's Legacy

BY NICOLE OLSTHOORN

It had taken me awhile to hear Her voice—or to understand who it was that was trying to speak to me and why. As a high-level medium, I had grown accustomed to communicating with Spirit Guides and other realms and dimensions. But She had felt different. More powerful. More demanding. Yet in a loving way.

In hindsight I can see it was Her who gave me the premonition I was going to die at the age of thirty-six. Who else could it be? Once I figured out who She was, it all made sense. She was the only one who could speak to me like that. Without words. Yet crystal clear. And when she did, well, those were the moments all doubts fell away. In those moments I just knew.

The premonition did not scare me. If fact, I was quite curious about life after death, so this didn't seem such a big deal. When I checked with my Spirit Guides how it was going to happen and they replied, "About something in your brain," I figured it to be a brain tumor of some sort. I never spoke to anyone about the premonition. It was none of their business, really. Plus that I suspected that not many around me would understand how I was able to live with this information. Most would probably worry. And I didn't want them to worry. The only one I ever shared it with was my dear friend and soul sister Joy.

"What do you mean you are going to die at thirty-six?" She asked with a comfortable mix of compassion and curiosity in her eyes.

I had wondered if she would think I was crazy if I told her what I knew. But there was no reason she would. She had always believed me. She had always been genuinely interested in what I had to share. So why would this be any different?

"I mean that for as long as I can remember, I have had this feeling that I would die at the age of thirty-six. Of something in my brain."

"You mean actually physically dying?"

"Yes."

"Why? Do you know that too?"

I had looked at her with great appreciation. Not only did she take me seriously, but she was also not afraid of talking about it. She was not afraid of asking the tough questions. And sometimes that was exactly what was needed for my psychic channel to open up and receive the answers. I could feel the familiar calmness, confidence, and certainty of Her in my body when I opened my mouth to voice Her answer: "I have come here to create a new world. To be a living, leading example of how beautiful life can be. But I am not going to stick around if no one is listening to me. If no one has eyes to see or ears to hear. If humanity is not up to speed with me by the time I am thirty-six, there is no point in me staying here. There is no point in hanging around."

Silence filled our campervan. Joy and I had not known each other for that long, but it felt as if we had shared lifetimes together. Only a few months ago I had received a vision of a house somewhere that I wanted to find. She had just decided to take a break from her life as she knew it. And together we had come up with a plan to hit the road and drive around Europe in a campervan for the winter. She looked at me with a cheeky glint in her eye: "Well," she said with the same sense of confidence as I had spoken Her words with, "humanity better hurry up then, 'cause it'd be their loss."

She was right. It would have been their loss. But that was not my default chain of thought at the time. During that conversation in the campervan a part of me still believed that there was something wrong with me. That people found me too deep, too intense, too emotional. And if I expressed all of that openly and freely they found me too loud and too obnoxious, too. For years I was told to "calm down," "not be so dramatic," and, the all-time favorite, "not take things so personal." What they and I both did not know, though, was that it was never personal. It was, in fact, far from personal. What I was feeling, sensing, and picking up on was something much greater than them or me combined. Something much more powerful. But no one knew. And so I concluded that me and my emotions took up too much of other people's time, space, and energy and that if I ever wanted to be accepted and live a somewhat normal life, it was in my favor to stay quiet and pretend I was not feeling anything at all anymore. Sugar did the trick, so I discovered. Especially chocolate and candy bars. So I ate them.

It did not take long for this suppression of my emotions to cause for an expansion of my body to an alarming 114 kilos (250 pounds). At my height, that weight officially classified as severely obese. Driven by this unconscious belief that I would be cast out if I were to express my true feelings, what had started as an innocent survival mechanism was now becoming an addiction on its own. Had I first felt my emotions were too much, I now concluded my physical presence was as well. Every evening I would stand in front of the mirror and tell myself I was fat and ugly. Plus that I found myself weak too for not being able to lose weight. "No wonder no man wants you," I would hiss to my mirror image. After which I would crawl into bed and cry myself to sleep. It was during these years that I received the premonition.

Along with the premonition I would also have returning dreams and visions of me with a slim and fit body dancing freely in a medium-size summer dress instead of XXXL. These psychic dreams and visions would be so real and so vivid that I would feel devastated as I re-emerged from them to reality. The gap between where I found myself and where I wanted to be was simply too big for me to hold space for. I figured that shedding the amount of weight I desired to shed would take years. And that idea alone was too much for me to bear. I wanted it fast. Like one-year-tops kind of fast. But my logical brain could not understand how sustainable weight loss could be achieved as fast as I desired it to be. This not-understanding had me in its grip. No matter how much thought I put into it, I just could not see the way. I couldn't figure it out. And so I ate more sugar to calm myself down.

That was, until I had a nervous breakdown and hit rock bottom and She was finally able to get through to me with a new vision. A different kind of vision. A vision that inspired hope instead of despair. A vision of a house.

"Time to go home," She had whispered gently without words.

And I had known. I had felt it. *She was right.*

Without hesitation, I sold my apartment, reduced all my belongings to one suitcase, and hit the road. I had no idea where this house was or how to get there. All I knew was that I had to find it. And so I went.

In hindsight, it is easy to see how it was a lack of faith and confidence in myself and me being good enough as I am that led me to block my natural psychic abilities and the receiving of clear guidance from something greater than me. Dreaming of the future, which always showed me as a slim woman, had simply been too confronting, too painful. As a result, I had lived my life in the past, while She had been patiently waiting for the moment I would give up my resistance so She would be able to pull me into my destined future again. Like a fire captured in smoldering rocks anticipating that one moment of fresh air to lighten it up, so too did She wait. It was not until I had that nervous breakdown that my logical brain was cracked open enough for me to receive this new vision of a house. Four months later, I was in the campervan with Joy.

Little did I know that this was just the tip of the iceberg. Her fire was now fueling an inner fire I never even realized was there. And it was burning in ways I didn't even know were possible. Everything that was not in alignment with Her deepest desires had to go, including the belief that I was too much. She made it clear that I had never been too much. I had simply been resonating with the painbody of the collective feminine. All the pain and fear of all women throughout all times and spaces had been raging through me. The intensity of it had been enormous. No wonder I had felt so incredibly overwhelmed! With Her now awake inside of me, this was changing. I was now starting to resonate with the collective feminine pleasure-body, too. This would soon balance the two out and lead me to transcend them both into Oneness.

She guided me home, my inner untamed self did. From The Netherlands, via France, Spain, and Greece, She guided me to England and then Wales. The moment I arrived on Celtic Land I knew this was where I belonged. This is where my new life was meant to be lived. By the time I officially filed the migration papers I had shed a total of 50 kilos (110 pounds) within a year and a half—something I had deemed impossible. She was fierce, strong, and confident in unapologetically going after what She wanted. If She had set her mind on something, it would happen. And I let Her. For the first time in my life, I let Her.

But it did not stop there.

Now that I had shed the weight and I had found the home I had set out to find, I started to realize that the real home She was guiding me to was the sacredness of my own body and the primal wild wisdom of my deepest desires. She helped me remember that I desired to dance around ancient stone circles, drink from holy springs, and visit sacred sites. That I longed to be a writer and a medium and to host retreats. That my heart was jumping with joy thinking of spreading the ancient faery magick of this part of the world all around the globe. She helped me remember that I desired to feel beautiful and to create beauty, to love and be loved in return. She helped me remember the dreams and desires I had forgotten. And then She showed me the most beautiful dream of all. The most sacred site I would ever visit. The holiest of springs I would ever drink from...My man.

Yet, on the morning of my thirty-fifth birthday, one year before I was supposed to die, all these newfound dreams and desires were yet to come into fruition. The stone circles were yet to be discovered and the sacred sites to be visited. The books were yet to be written and the retreats set up. The faery magick was yet to be channeled and the man to be attracted. And with only one year to go, how was this all going to happen? And if this was all going to happen, how was I going to fully enjoy and experience all of that with so little time left?

As I woke that morning, I had asked Her: "If I really have just one more year to live, what would I do?"

With loving certainty, She had said: "I would leave a legacy."

And I had known. As always when She spoke, I had known. *She was right.*

For two decades I had thought of myself as being too much for this world. Too deep. Too intense. Too emotional. Too big. For two decades I had felt guilty for taking up the space I was taking—in energy at first and in physical form later. My obese body had been a perfect reflection of that inner world.

But that body was no longer there. The dreams and visions I had of myself being slim and fit had become a physical reality. The weight had come off surprisingly effortlessly and in record time, just like I had always sensed it was supposed to. And the amount of weight that had come off equaled a whole person.

Her premonition was never about dying. It was about living. It was about me allowing my mind to be cracked open so that Her wild wisdom could be unleashed. It was about me restoring my faith in that wild wisdom. In Her visions. Her nudges. Her hunches. And in myself and my ability to act on them. I had given myself to Her. And She had taken me, turned me on, and brought me back to life. And now She would let me die? Of course not! She would not let me die. Quite the opposite. She had made sure that all the parts of me that had wanted to die had died. All the parts of me that felt too much for this world had left. Including the weight. And She had done all that so that we could live. Not die. Live.

Tears welled up when a deep appreciation and gratitude for my life sank in.

"What kind of legacy?" I asked Her.

But there was only one legacy to live really. Only one way forward. The Wild Wisdom Way of Her, my untamed Divine Feminine. I had unleashed Her. I had surrendered myself to Her. To Her fire. Her Wildness. Her Wisdom. She was *speaking* me. *Writing* me. *Living* me. There was no way back. She had become me. And I had become Her. I had even taken on Her name: The Celtic Goddess.

As the first rays of sunlight had started to beam through the cracks of my curtains that day, so too beamed Her light through every cell of my body. The familiar calmness, confidence, and certainty filled me up from within when Her loving confirming answer found its way into my consciousness: "The legacy you died for darling, the legacy you died for."

I don't know where I am going,
all I know is where I have been.
And how it feels underneath this skin.

I don't know who I am becoming,
but I am certain who I am.
And who I am is wild and free
far beyond your plan.

—Jai Jagdeesh, lyrics from "She Kissed Me"

With an impressive record of defying the status quo of what is possible by following your inner voice, high-level medium and spiritual teacher **Nicole Olsthoorn** is an upcoming international author, unleashing the inner voices of women and men worldwide by helping them enhance their natural psychic abilities.

Nicole has been a teacher for spirited women CEOs, managers and business owners from all over the globe, reaching out to her from the US, Canada, Scandinavia, The Netherlands, Belgium and the UK longing to build, strengthen and expand their business from a sense of purpose and a deeper connection to (their) Spirit.

After years of sharing her enlightening teachings with them one-on-one and in private groups only, she is now making her vast knowledge of co-creation with Spirit(s) available for a wider audience through a unique blend of live and online experiences.

Combining her love for ancient Celtic wisdom with her contagious enthusiasm for the conscious evolution of humanity and the enlightenment of our planet as a whole, her work is drenched in channeled wisdom from ancient natural worlds as well as a deep understanding and embodiment of the Infinite Source of Divine Loving Presence that we all are.

With her gentle, kind and reassuring approach she leaves those who choose to connect with her bathing in a soothing embrace of unconditional love, pristine clarity and a joyful encouragement to turn inwards, recognize the truth of Who And What They Are and find the courage to unleash the voice of their own inner wild wisdom, too. Learn more at **www.nicoleolsthoorn.com.**

Special Gift

WILD WISDOM ACTIVATION EXERCISE

Stop suppressing. Start unleashing.

Download your free Wild Wisdom Activation Exercise at
www.nicoleolsthoorn.com/freegiftsetsail

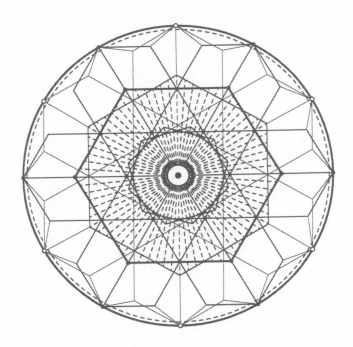

The Science of Happiness

BY DR. DAVIA SHEPHERD

This is a "how to" guide: How to live your optimal life, live longer, healthier and happier, and at all costs avoid burnout. But it starts with a tale of burnout and the need for balance. This is my story. I'm a physician. I should have known better; I should have seen the signs. But you know what they say: It's hard to see the picture when you are standing in the frame.

My dad was less than perfect, but he was smart and driven. He and his team had made a scientific discovery that has helped the world, and when I was as young as six, he would ask me and my sister what our contribution to the world would be. Back then, my signature contribution was playing with my Barbies. But, come career decision time, his words somehow stuck in my head and I knew that whatever I ended up doing, it had to be something important. The seed had been planted.

All my life I was taught to work hard to achieve. I was taught at home and by life that I had to give it my all and to work harder than everyone else just to be recognized. And so I did. I did pretty well in school, showed an aptitude for science, and ended up on the medical school track just like every immigrant parent hopes for their kids. Keep working hard: Good girl. Study hard: Good girl. Long nights, overnights, burning the candle at both ends...but I was a model student and a model daughter...and I was living the dream, right?

Even though I now work in patient care, I never thought I'd end up here. I started off thinking I was going to be the kind of doctor who never actually saw patients. Research was my jam. I wanted to discover or at least work on the development of a drug that would change the world, cure something that would be meaningful to a lot of people. Maybe have my name on a new drug box.

I worked in the pharmaceutical industry for years, and I did pretty well there. But my first taste of burnout may have started there, too. The long hours, late nights, and weekends spent doing things I was less than passionate about while "paying dues," as they say, may probably have led to burnout...but something unexpected happened. At the rate I was going I could have hit rock bottom, but that wouldn't happen for years to come. By a stroke of luck, something occurred that I didn't think fortunate at the time. It changed my whole career trajectory.

I know you hear enough about the big bad pharmaceutical industry. My job here is not to vilify the industry at all. I think drugs are great as long as we aren't overusing them and are using them appropriately. Technological advances in medicine over the years have been amazing and life-changing in many ways, and there is also a lot of room for improvement. I want to say this in the best way possible because I want you to understand that there are men and women who work in pharma who have their hearts in the right place, and they are committed to helping, but this is my story. I witnessed and experienced some things that did not mesh with my values, I had a crisis of conscience and left big pharma to pursue a holistic option.

There I was with my new big dream of being a holistic physician, but, my background had absolutely nothing to do with treating patients holistically. I'm a lifelong learner so my next step was obvious to me. I went back to school as a "mature" student. Being a student is challenging enough when you are the same age as everyone else!

I'm from an immigrant family. My parents are Jamaican, and you may have heard the running joke about Jamaicans: they all have five jobs! When I went back to school as a mature student I had only two part-time jobs in addition to being a full-time student. The running joke at family gatherings was: "Only two jobs? What an underachiever!"

In my life growing up, having a strong work ethic was drilled into me. That was by no means a bad thing—up to a point. Certain beliefs were ingrained into my psyche, such as: "You have to work hard for every cent of your salary," and "Toil through the night." "No pain, no gain," was another one you may have heard growing up, too. I could list a hundred of these sayings. My parents meant well. They had worked hard to achieve what they had. You can only teach what you know, and under the circumstances they were doing the very best they could. Through my own experiences I learned a little differently, and I share that with my kids every chance I get.

I'm sure growing up that my parents' intention was to motivate me into doing something with my life, to live up to the potential they could see in me, but one thing I can tell you for sure is that there was no balancing voice encouraging self-care and self-love during my journey through childhood. I believe that it's that lack of balance that got me to the point of not being able to walk, being on crutches, and still being in the office treating patients. But I'm getting ahead of myself in this story.

I've learned to be a giver. To give of myself, of my time, of my resources. Part of that may just be my natural personality. I'm truly happy giving. Part of it may have been my programming: "It is better to give than to receive," was interpreted by my child mind as "Give everything, give your all, and also receiving is bad." It's not what the saying means, but it's how I internalized it. You've also probably heard "Cast your bread on the water and it will be returned to you..." I can tell you I did not focus on the returned to you part, I was all about the casting...and casting...and casting...

I know that I'm not the only one. I know that there are many of us, especially in the service professions. We live to serve. We give and give and give some more. We work way into the night. We would give the coat off our backs in a winter storm so someone else could be a little more comfortable, and we do it with no expectation of anything in return, we do it happily. And that's okay, even commendable, but we run into trouble if we lack the key element of balance.

You may be wondering, when did her burnout actually occur? Was it when she went back to school with a daily long commute (sometimes over three hours depending on traffic), working two jobs, seven days a week? Nope. I was doing pretty well with that. I was fine! I was studying an area of medicine that filled me with joy and hope for the future of mankind. My body was pumping dopamine and serotonin all day every day. I was ready to take on the world, and I did, and I did great. There *was* balance. I was giving a lot of me, but I was also getting back so many rewards that I was positively shining. School was challenging, but I thrived on every opportunity to expand my knowledge and learn something new. I recently attended a workshop where the speaker led us in a character strengths-finder exercise, and my number-one strength was "love of learning." I could never burn out in school. But then I was thrust back in the real world and that's when I fell—hard.

Here's how it happened. I was now officially a grownup. School was behind me, I was working in private practice, I had a house, a family, a baby...all that grown-up stuff. (I will preface this by saying I love my *Lovie*. He is everything, but as a baby, he never slept.)

I went back to work when my baby was six weeks old. I would get up, drop him off with Grandma (shout out to all the granny nannies) go to work, pick him up after work, and then he would be up every two hours all night long. I nursed past two years old, so when he got up at night, I was it.

I know you are shouting at the page about all the things I could have done better in terms of sleep training, but I didn't know any of that stuff. All I knew was that my baby cried, he needed me and I was up. I love him so much. He finally slept through the night when he was eighteen months old. I still remember the first night like it was yesterday. I was terrified because I thought there was something wrong. For many nights I would get up, listen to the baby monitor, stealthily peek in his crib to make sure he was breathing and then drop back into bed. To say I was exhausted would be an understatement. I feel as though the lexicon needs a new word to explain what I was experiencing! But faithfully, every day I would get up and repeat the process. With all that cortisol coursing through my body constantly and with the constant lack of sleep, the crash was inevitable.

As I said, I'm a physician. I should have seen it coming, but the truth is, I *totally* did not. I kept wondering why I wasn't losing the baby weight like I anticipated. I was eating a very good diet, I was getting exercise, and I was nursing. Surely the pounds should just melt off, right? But, they weren't budging. Nothing was happening and so in my infinite wisdom I decided (with everything else I had going on) to ramp up my exercise schedule and train for the Hartford Marathon. It was great, it was fun, I made new friends, we started a run team in or practice, and we raised money for a worthy cause. All great stuff. But with me eating very few calories per day and not sleeping at night something had to give—and *give it did.*

I have always been a little bit on the sensitive side. As a child I was diagnosed with airway inflammation and skin inflammation disorders, but over the years I had gotten those things under control. I spent the majority of my older life as a paragon of health and wellness. After I ran the marathon relay, I suddenly started having really weird, wonderful, and dare I say, a little bit *gross* symptoms. I was freaked out; I didn't know what was going on with me. I went to urgent care one day when the pain was particularly severe, and they sent me to a surgi-center where I was mis-diagnosed and had a completely unnecessary minor surgery performed which did nothing to help my condition and only made things worse. I went to my primary care physician and he didn't have any idea what was going on with me. He referred me to another specialist, but I didn't keep the appointment. I was way too busy. Plus, at this point I had seen four different providers and I was only getting worse.

I was in the office one afternoon smiling at patients through the pain as I hobbled on crutches, trying to help everyone else's pain (I know, the irony is not lost on me) when the voice of God through one of my patients said: "Doc, you have to go take care of yourself." It was my doctor-heal-thyself moment.

Never had I left work early or canceled patient appointments because of my needs, and I had certainly never closed our office. But that day my feet felt as though they were on fire, and I just couldn't go any more. I called the specialist and explained my emergency and they saw me right away. It helped that, as a physician, I got in that quickly, it also helped that my very kind primary care doctor at the time made a call to the specialist who was a friend of his to get me seen immediately.

I've worked in teaching hospitals and teaching clinics over my almost twenty years in healthcare, and I know that when your specialist calls in the other docs and the students, well, let's just say your condition is a tad serious? After much poking and prodding, someone said, "It must be auto-immune." *Finally* I was able to take my blinders off and see what was going on with me. At that point I knew exactly what I needed to do. I would treat myself exactly the same way I would treat my own patient.

This story has a happy ending. By marrying functional medicine and traditional medicine methods, within six months I was well on the way to recovery. I have a diagnosis, but I know it's not my destiny. That was almost a decade ago, and I have had just two flare-ups, including one when I had my second baby. He, too, wouldn't sleep through the night until he was eighteen months. I had again neglected self-care and so it was no surprise that the symptoms showed up. The key is that getting back to my regimen gets me back on track.

I'll share with you the science of happiness. Being a recovering researcher, I look at the body as a big chemistry set, a metabolic puzzle, if you will. For most of us, if we can get the big pieces to function well together we do pretty well health-wise and also as far as happiness goes. The four-part plan that I like to recommend has been a lifesaver for me and for many of our patients.

If we can get our bodies to produce what I call the happy hormones more of the time and less of the ones that put us in a state of fight and flight, our overall health and wellness—physically, emotionally, and mentally—improves tremendously. Increasing healthy activities that increase sero-tonin, dopamine, endorphins, and oxytocin and decreasing the drivers of cortisol and adrenaline helps the body function optimally.

There's lots of overlap here, but I routinely mention diet, not in the sense of losing weight, but more along the lines of eating to reduce inflammation and based on your unique make-up. It's not a one-size-fits-all process.

Anyone who tells you to just eat right and exercise isn't looking at the whole picture. I also like to focus on the fact that what we put in our body is just as important as what we use in our environments and also on our bodies. Traditional approaches are still catching up to this idea, but patients find it makes a difference.

The fourth piece of the puzzle as I see it is balance. Not just work-life balance, but figuring out what really lights you up, and then making a living doing that. Working smarter, not harder. Leaning away from the "I have to do it all myself" model and more into the "together we go farther" model. Self-care, a sense of community, stress relief, and some acknowledgment of something bigger seems to be the way to go.

I'm a huge fan of a little TV show called "Star Trek—The Next Generation." There was a doctor on that show who may or may not have influenced me in my pursuit of health and wellness. I'm always looking for new ways to help, the cutting-edge technologies. My mission, should I choose to accept it, and as I see it, is to help women live their optimal lives. Why women? Women are the moms, the grandmas, the aunties, the sisters, the friends, the lovers, the wives, the girlfriends...need I go on? How will we get this message out to the world? It's going to be by sharing with people who are receptive. Yes, we can live longer, healthier happier lives. Yes, we can have better quality of life and fewer incidences of the so-called lifestyle and autoimmune diseases that are the number-one causes of morbidity in the United States.

"What? Live longer you say?"

"Yep! I said that!"

"Healthier and happier too?"

"Ah-huh!"

"Nope, I have enough of that thanks very much," said...*no one ever!*

History shows that prior to around 1900 if you lived past sixty-five you were considered positively ancient. With the advent of simple changes, such as washing our hands, we added almost twenty years to our life expectancies. That's amazing. But, with the increase in industrialization and food processing came the lifestyle diseases. So now we do live longer, but our quality of life suffers. Almost everyone I know knows someone whose family is affected by Alzheimer's or some other form of dementia. Heart disease and cancer are so common, if you mention to someone that you have that diagnosis, they might start telling you about their similar diagnosis. The statistics look grim.

But what if we could, over the next ten years, change the statistics? In the 1900s we changed the world by cleaning up our external environment. What if just by cleaning up our *internal environment*—mind and body—we could make that leap to adding the life back to our years?

I'm committed to that future, and I invite you to join me.

Dr. Davia H. Shepherd MPhil, MS, DC has had a varied career in healthcare spanning Biochemistry, Pharmacology, and Holistic Health. She is the founder and CEO of Power-Transformations, a breakthrough platform that dares to look at health and wellness completely differently from the traditional approach. Her focus is on what ideal, optimal health looks like for you, and then, using state of the art tools and gold standard processes, a customized solution is developed specifically for you.

Dr. Shepherd believes that having your ideal weight, size, energy levels, physical health, and mental sharpness is absolutely possible, not only now but well into your 90s. One of her favorite sayings is, "We do not have to decline as we get older". Instead of a "one size fits all" approach, her proven 4-step protocol gets outstanding individualized results for her clients, that continue as one ages gracefully. If you have ever thought that you would love to live a healthier, longer, quality filled life but that somehow the traditional methods haven't worked or just don't seem to go far enough, then you and Dr. Davia are of the same mindset. She's been through her own struggles, both with her health and with the healthcare system as a whole, thus inspiring her to focus on prevention rather than band-aid solutions.

She lives in Connecticut with super-husband Wayne and her two small children and is just a short drive from the support of the Granny Nannies, Cherry and Vivian.

For more about Dr. Davia and Power-Transformations please visit **www.Power-Transformations.com.**

Special Gift

OPTIMAL WELLNESS BREAKTHROUGH SESSION
(VALUE $497)

Are you the kind of person who would rather prevent rather than cure an illness or disorder? If you have ever felt that you would like to live a longer, healthier, and happier life, If optimal sounds great to you and just okay (or less than okay,) sounds like a terrible idea, then I welcome you to your very own Optimal Wellness Breakthrough.

This 1-hour session is completely devoted to outlining a plan for you to get from "okay to optimal". We will explore what you most want now and what's really important for you in your current and future health and wellness. We will look at where you are right now and explore the gap between where you are and where you want to be. At that point, I'll recommend some concrete next steps for you depending on what you most need.

To take advantage of your complimentary session, please go to **www.wellnessbreakthroughcall.com** and select your optimal time. Or just call us in office 860-589-1491 to schedule.

Regards in health!

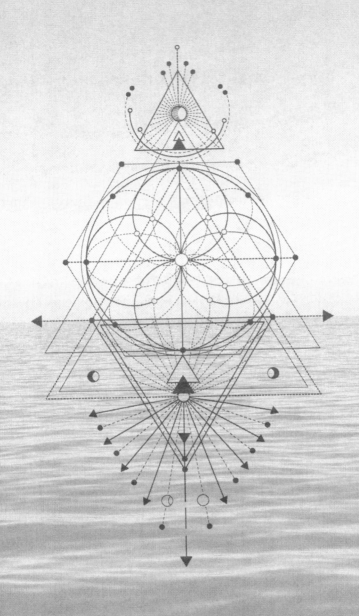

Wild Love

BY DANA ELAINE SCHLICK

Death has been my teacher.

First, not by choice. Then, still not by conscious choice. And recently, I chose. "Are you willing?", my soul asks. "Are you willing to let go and trust the wildness of love?" I willingly let go...saying yes to the unknown. Trusting my soul's knowing of the way it needs to go—even when what I have been asked to let go of is so incredibly precious.

This radical trust is the legacy of love gifted through loss. Though the willingness to let go has not come easy.

This is my story of falling. Of facing my shadow until the darkness was made sweet.

> "When love beckons to you, follow him,
> Though his ways are hard and steep...
> And think not you can direct the course
> of love, for love, if it finds you worthy,
> directs your course."
>
> —Kahlil Gibran on Love, *The Prophet*

DESCENT

I went down. Down the spiral path into the world of deep feeling. The world of demons and gems. To face, to feel and to discover my soul. The underworld strips you bare. Once naked, it cuts you to the bone. To be carved out is painful. Skinned of falsehoods and perceptions of control. Few go down—even fewer go willingly.

This is where life initiated me. "Now." She commanded. "Go."

Many live in the in-between—clawing into the ledge, refusing to go, exhausting themselves in the resistance.

Wise words spoken: "If you're going through hell, keep going".

I've known this clinging—absolute terror, shame, panic and shut down when my shadow said "hello" in full force. I began to get hints at age thirteen, when deeply disillusioned by my dearest, attached-at-the-hip friend. My heart was broken repeatedly from betrayals. But I managed to dodge the full initiation by transcending into angelic realms and gratitude.

But at sixteen years old, I was dragged down with no escape. I had begun smoking marijuana and she parted the veils, stripping my defenses so I could fully *feel what was real*—the delight, but mostly the depth of pain in myself and the world—and it was overwhelming. I was living the mythic descent of Persephone. The young Greek goddess whose innocent beauty tantalized the god of the underworld, leading him to crack the earth open as she picked wildflowers, forcing her to marry him (the darkness). However, at the time I had no context for my new reality. All the ways I knew myself and how to relate to others—gone. And I was not prepared.

My ability to stave off the descent by bypassing into positivity shattered. I went from social butterfly to barely being able to leave my house. My nervous system was swinging from panic to shut down—in search of safety—with no success.

This cycle went on for years. I never knew when it would happen, or for how long. Sometimes it lasted ten days, other times, ten months. As inexplicably as I'd be pulled down, I would pop back up to the land of the living. I didn't understand. I was well loved—my nickname was sunshine!—but something mysterious overpowered me. I was initiated into the darkness, and life would never be the same.

Even with my damnedest of efforts my reality could not be changed. My will was strong. My thinking, hopeful. Psychiatrists, therapists, medications, diagnosis after diagnosis... "Severe depression and anxiety", I was told—a life sentence of unfortunate genes to only be managed by medication. At first I was relieved to have a name for this hell, but very quickly my soul rebelled. I knew nothing was inherently wrong with me, though I feared it all the while. The shame was heavy. Relationships suddenly interrupted as I was unable to express what was happening. My dreams and ability to create my desired life were frozen in time. I felt imprisoned by an experience that no one else could see.

I'd take refuge at the pristine black beach bluffs during college. I'd gaze into the deep-blue horizon waters with the glistening golden sand under my feet. Watching how it would all cease to shine with sundown. It was here, in the quietest moments of listening, I learned to hear the whispering of my soul, *"There is beauty in the darkness—it's just harder to see."*

I continued my search to understand this darkness. It was all that truly mattered, my life depended on it.

The fires of this pain were building a strength from the core, of the core. Every time I was languishing, writhing in agony fighting to feel differently, my soul's capacity to endure—increased. Paradoxically, exhausting my grip.

Until a moment of grace allowed me to fully surrender to my experience. Suddenly and swiftly, I'd be buoyed back up to breathe, reminding me, *"Let go. Be Caught. It's only an abyss when you forget you can fly."*

Growing in confidence from my newfound buoyancy, I joined a yoga community devoted to Divine Light. As the light intensified, I felt a childlike animation of life return. And with it, the shadow to match. This experience was like no other. As the expansion increased, the fear came with it. The leadership naively told me to continue to "Turn to the light"—leading to a multiple week experience of the greatest terror of my life. I felt as if I was floating above my body and the earth, tethered to reality only by a thin, thin string. My soul was not in my body.

Forced to return home, I attempted to put the pieces together: yes, my family had dysfunction; yes, my father could be intimidating; and *after* these trauma reactions began, yes, I was sexually assaulted multiple times in my late teens.

Still, this level of terror did not match my life story. It felt beyond me—existential, collective and archetypal—though living in me as sensations in my body. I surrendered the need to know, acknowledging my body was making sense for whatever it was holding. Again, I learned to listen: *"Wait, and feel the weight of your body. You can only go as quickly as the slowest part of you."* Over time, as I slowed, I digested these sensations. One by one, I began to land back home in my body and on earth, vowing to stay firmly rooted.

The many spiral journeys down and back gifted me a depth of beauty and contact with my soul I could not have imagined. And still, the fear of the unknown—and getting dragged down again—lingered.

OCEAN OF LOVE

At age twenty-five, as I entered graduate school in hope of helping others from my journey, I met a man.

Synchronicities strung together from the moment I laid my eyes on his chest: the number of my dinner ticket that night was blazoned on his ironic t-shirt "69". I was immediately drawn to him, but he didn't respond as I was used to. I assumed he wasn't interested. Later, as I observed the house party, his first words to me were: "There's a part of you that is innocent, and a part that is wise from pain".

He felt me. He saw me.

Mike had a handlebar mustache he would wax into place. He was a passionate singer-songwriter with piercing, poetic lyrics and a Spanish guitar. Physically, the strongest person I had ever known, skillfully traversing trails and roads on his mountain bike and motorcycle.

I alluded to past pain with men when I had felt objectified and consent wasn't given. So when I froze and left my body during our first sexual union—I was thrown back into the underworld. Mike reached out with care, saying he valued our connection even if it didn't involve sexuality. The sincerity of his love touched me deeply and we were together from that moment on—three years and a season.

He embodied the energy of his namesake, Archangel Michael. He told me how he valued protecting those he loved. I scoffed in my learned self-reliance, "What if someone doesn't need to be protected?"

I never realized how much I needed this all my life.

His presence liberated a deeper relaxation inside of me, even as I continued to dip into the underworld again and again. He showed up, again and again, patiently listening, holding me, assuring me he never wanted to take anything from me that I couldn't freely give.

I brought him to those black beach bluffs to let him in on the beauty and aloneness I had felt many years prior. He looked at me unwavering: "Do you feel alone now?" This realization penetrated deep into my cells. "No", I replied, as tears streamed down my sun-warmed face.

I showed him my most vulnerable and ashamed parts, and he loved them. He showed me his, and I loved them. The freeze in my system was melting, and our love deepening every day.

On a December winter night, as we embraced in our bed, it felt like our love expanded through galaxies...the gratitude overflowing in our recognition of finding each other. I was never more content, never more at home.

The next sunny afternoon, he was struck on his motorcycle.

It was a miracle he survived the crash. He lost a lot of blood. First, his leg was amputated. We were told it would be a marathon of recovery. That night as I lay waiting with his mother in prayer, I pulled the goddess oracle cards: *Trust, True Love, Undying Love.*

Thirteen hours later, he was declared non-responsive. I had to ask the doctor many times what he meant by *"non-responsive"*. He was gone.

As I took a walk through the hospital grounds with my mother, the white roses were distant, the blue sky—flat. It dawned on me that his soul knew this would happen. He'd open his sets with the Dolly Parton cover "Jolene, Jolene, I'm begging of you please don't take my man. Jolene, Jolene, please don't take him just because you can."

Jolene was the name of the woman who struck him.

His songs were guidance for the journey.

I had three days by his side as preparation began for his organs to be donated. Even in his death he was generous. I asked everyone to relate to him as alive, as I continued to hold hope a miracle could happen. I played our favorite music, as friends and family came and went.

As I stood by his bedside, and as people commented on what a tragedy it was, I felt a strange grace.

Before I had to say goodbye, a nurse suggested I lay by his side. I disrobed into a hospital gown to be skin-to-skin with him one more time. Moments later, the nurse rushed in, startled.

My heartbeat was being picked up on his heart monitor.

I don't know how I walked out of that room, but as I did there was a watercolor angel pinned on the wall with the word "Trust" underneath her.

The absence of his presence was profound. His jokes that would sometimes take minutes to the get the full depth of wit, the impersonations only he could make (often of me as Glenda the Good Witch behind my back), his bluesy harmonica wafting through our home, the generosity of his undivided presence, his soulful amber eyes and quick smile, his embrace that penetrated my soul, and his cowboy boots with separating soles beside our bed, so grand...and so empty.

It felt as though I had been preparing my whole life for this to happen. I learned to let people witness my pain. I had a repeated crash-course in surrendering to things out of my control. And now a whole new remembrance of the necessity of ritual.

I had a knowing of the need for ritual at his bedside. I had a knowing to be witnessed as I entered my home for the first time upon returning from the hospital—not just by my mother but by my whole community. I had a knowing for many rituals. So, I created and found rituals: by myself, ones I invited others to join, and community rituals.

I learned my grief and need for ritual to honor and heal was not for everyone. My grief touched on others' grief that was not ready to be faced and released.

Nonetheless I loved my tears...the aliveness, the pleasure of expressing this love filled me. Mike became a bridge of safety to the spirit world and to feel it all.

I knew the depth of my grief was the depth of my love. And I let it pour. I descended again into the underworld—but this time, in an entirely different way. I was met with an ocean of love.

The home we created with our love, became the ocean for all the waters of grief to flow into—sometimes they were trickles, tributaries, and quiet streams, but many times they were raging rivers and waterfalls of force.

Six months after he passed, shame from my desire to connect with men sooner than I imagined, and fear that my loyalty to Mike would be questioned—overtook me just as I was about to leave for my first foreign adventure since a young teen. I had put my dreams to travel on hold, out of fear of never knowing when the underworld experience would come. And now both were here.

I'd often put my music on shuffle allowing spirit to speak, and Mike often spoke through the songs that came on. Music was so central to him and to our connection. So many times, the exact song and lyrics would shuffle on to share a message.

This night, as I packed, a random audiobook called *Radical Acceptance* began to play in my music library. I'd never heard it before. As Tara spoke of befriending all emotion, and I practiced with her guidance, the freeze began to thaw out. I stayed up all night as feeling washed through me, moment-to-moment allowing the emotion—energy in motion—to move.

It continued non-stop. As I sat on the back of the plane, in between my friend and mother, the tears flowed. At times they turned into grand shaking, deep sobbing, and I just let them—seeping into parts that longed to be touched by love. I felt the grace as I let these beloved women hold my process with protection and care as flight stewards and passengers passed. This active allowing continued for the next several days. I knew something had deeply changed. I went through the fire with the waters of my grief and emerged a different woman. I was facing every visitor—terror, despair, shame, longing—with resiliency, and coming through.

During this trip I faced and took pleasure in the triggers that would normally have taken me down—and flew. A new path of freedom was forged. I came home transformed.

Mike told me I was one of the strongest people he had ever known. The underworld tempered me. Months before his death, we purchased a dancing skeleton bride and groom painting, titled, "I can handle it." I hated this title. I was tired of enduring pain. But it was accurate of what was to come.

I came to understand how his soul knew I could stand by his side through his death, and receive the fullness of his sacrifice.

This fierce gift of love caught the threads of what seemed like lifetimes of frozen grief in my nervous system, in my ancestry, and in the world—

cleansing, healing, and weaving each thread back with each sacred tear and roar—into a quilt of wholeness and belonging.

Letting love have her wild, wild way freed me from the underworld suffering that had gripped me for thirteen years.

In Mike's first love song to me, his voice rang:

"We both know freedom comes at a price, I'll pay it, for you, without thinking twice. Even if it must, It must, be the end of you and me. You shall be free. Darling I dare you put steel in your eyes and let your freedom ring...ring...ring."

COMING BACK TO LIFE

13 has been a key number. At 13-years old, the underworld began to knock. In the 13th hour, Mike was struck. Thirteen hours after the crash, his brain died. On the 13th day of December 2013 his heart stopped beating. Culminating in 13 years in the underworld before my freedom.

Largely misunderstood and demonized, 13 is the Death card in the Tarot, symbolizing absolute transformation.

A little over a year after Mike passed, my heart and body opened to love again, on Friday the 13th. And as I write this now, it is again Friday the 13th, on a full moon—a very rare occurrence (the next one is in 30 years).

I met Maxwell at a music show. His brother, coincidentally named Mike, introduced us. Maxwell was easy to talk to. As the show was to end and he began to leave, my body instinctively summoned him back with a come-hither finger. He looked behind to see if I was motioning someone else. Later that night, with easy tears, I shared with him where I was, allowing him in on my grief and love. He was present and didn't flinch. We made love that night. He paused as he held my hips with such reverence and desire, commenting, "You are such a woman." I knew what he meant. I was no longer a girl, or young woman. I am woman.

Grief broke the seed of my sexuality open, watered it and now was coming into blossom.

Maxwell was a lover of all things real. He was an artisan builder by trade who reveled in the raw beauty of wood and stone, adventurer of wild lands and waters, and passion-fueled man that made me a bed made entirely from an old-world temple door. He had been a young father, like my beloved Mike, now with two adolescents, and in a parallel process of grieving, as he navigated the separation of his family with a recent divorce.

I hesitated to open. Was I really ready? So I broke it off. Several months later, when my favorite astrologer predicted "Love Calls," Maxwell rang. I knew I had to answer. He challenged me: "Will you love someone here on earth?"

His question got me lit, tempting me to explain how love does not die when a human body does.

But I was quieted as I felt his question coming from a place far beyond his personal desire—smashing my imagined timelines of readiness. My soul was stirred to come back to life.

My whole being swelled with Maxwell, the connection felt ancient, and somehow I knew I would have to let him go at a not-so-distant future.

Love asked, *"Are you willing to know the tenderness and fragility of love and bleed willingly? Joyfully?"*

Maxwell asked, "Can we go too far?"

He knew the risk. I replied, "Is there a *too far?*" I would jump if he was willing to jump with me.

Like his family name, our connection was spoon-feeding me back to life. The inner conflict of loyalty to Mike emerged. But when I sensed in, Mike's message was clear: "Love. This is how you share the glory of our love. You have so much to give. This is how you honor me... Leap."

So I leaped—as I shared "I love you." Maxwell looked on with widened but composed eyes.

I said it for love's sake. I never felt so free. As my heart grew wings, simultaneously, my heart broke open in grief—making room for this new love to enter. My bittersweet tears filling in the cracks—like Japanese artisans rejoin broken pottery with gold—with the precious recognition, that this too, will change.

As I opened my heart, I challenged his full presence and heart in our lovemaking. He challenged me to come fully into my body and raw expression. The deeper we touched into places of pain with love, we were skyrocketed into pleasure. The bed became the healing ground, where the many waters of grief and ecstasy flowed.

I ebbed and flowed with Maxwell for over four years, like the ancient dance of the caduceus snakes that comes apart and together many times and meets at the crown. I separated with him for short periods, as tension grew with my soul's need of temperance.

I listened to my soul, even when I didn't want to. Each time so hard to let go, each time intending it was the end, each time leading us back to each other—and each time, so essential. I realized we were both easing the pain of parting, through this gradual transition. With every goodbye, it was freeing the totality of grief's expression, lightening the heaviness, and sharpening my ability to consciously let go. I'd be in full-on snotty sobs then shift into full-on belly laughter. This was not transcendence. This was alchemy—my body in full union with my soul.

Many times, life wielded the sword for me—stripping and cutting away what was most precious.

Now Death asked, *"Will you do the wielding?"*

So I simply said "Yes"—repeatedly, as Maxwell asked a series of sincere and direct questions: "Are you sure you want me to stop fighting for this? Are you sure you want to end this?..."

I wielded the sword. The sword that was so kind and so deadly. With a slice that was clear and still stings.

Love and death taught me mysteries I am still learning. Love is not ever-expanding life. Love is letting go—surrendering to the full spiral dance of creation—breath-by-breath, day-to-night, season-into-season.

Deeply enamored, yet unintentionally named after the Monarch butterfly, *Danaus Plexippus,* the queen of life, death, and rebirth has knocked at the door of my soul asking, *"Are you willing? Are you willing to let go and trust the wildness of love?"*

"Yes. Teach me Love. Direct my course."

Dana Elaine Schlick is a licensed psychotherapist, energy healer, and community ritualist. She believes in the transformative power, fierce grace, and aliveness that is gifted from fully feeling. She is emerging from deep life initiations to breathe beauty into her new edge: creative expression of her inner world. She began writing in devotion to share this story that had to be told. You can connect with Dana at **withwildlove. com** or instagram: with.wild.love

Special Gift

FREE AUDIO VERSION OF "WILD LOVE"

One woman's journey about how the fierce gift of love alchemized lifetimes of frozen grief and wove each thread of aliveness into a quilt of wholeness and belonging.

Access here: **www.withwildlove.com/setsail**

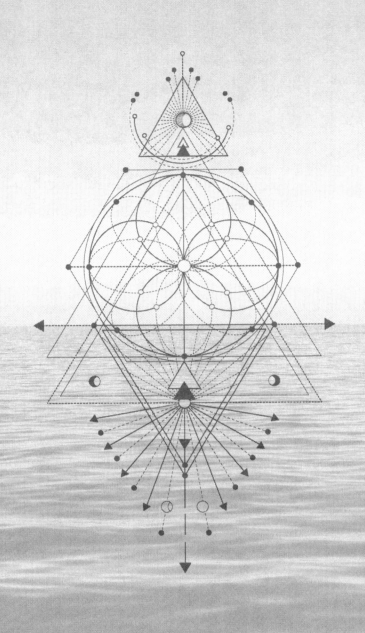

Easy Joy: Remembering the "More" of Who We Are

BY ADRIANNE SPIRALLIGHT

"Elephants."
What? I keep walking.
"Elephants."

I stop and turn around. I'm standing alone on an inexplicably empty patch of hot, dirty, cracked and crowded Thirteenth Street sidewalk. There is no one close enough to have spoken to me. I shake my head and resume my stride. Abruptly, I am jarred to a halt again, this time by a booming *tick-tick-tick* echoing loudly in my head, as if the white rabbit himself were flattening his pocket watch against my ear. "Elephants. Elephants never forget."

I am six years old, standing in the summer sun on a newly blacktopped driveway, trying to scrape tar off my faded and patchy carnation pink ball. I look up to the sky suddenly and say, "Oh!" Then I smile.

"Sorry," a woman mutters as she bumps past me. Thirteenth Street swims back into my perception in all its steamy, crushing, horn-honking blare. I stand there, swaying and blinking in the bright light, swerving pedestrians swearing at me.

Elephants, I whisper to myself. *Elephants never forget.* But I did.

At first, it was just memories of a memory. It was me, at twenty-six, surfing hazy waves of recall, remembering me, at six, remembering that moment, holding it close like a treasure, excited to share the wealth, and thinking, *I understand now. I understand it all now and I'll never forget.* Sometimes, I can still feel the shock of that memory, how it catalyzed an instantaneous recalibration of self, startling me into awareness of an intriguing other, perhaps truer, me, existing invisibly right alongside the one I recognized and performed every day.

Like the afternoon, a month or so into my freshman year of college, when I bounced into the ID checkpoint at my dorm and spent thirty minutes chatting with the security guard and the other students who came through, before I headed to my room. Halfway up the stairs, the walls of my mind were suddenly splashed with enormous, red, neon graffiti letters: I'm not shy! I just spent half an hour idly talking to strangers—I'm not organically, unalterably shy!

In that gray, institutional-concrete stairwell, my psyche was granted reprieve from the life sentence of solitary confinement my misguided family had unjustly pronounced upon me—and I, having no other guidance, had accepted. It was a joyous release.

So I was familiar with the phenomenon of discovering that I'd always been someone other than who I had been told I was. But this was different. This was mysterious. This held vast implications, extending, perhaps, beyond my own private life. Yet, as much as my astounded adult-self wanted to re-collect every part of what I knew at six, I also felt an unsettling hesitation. Like an in-rushing wave with an unseen undertow moves powerfully forward and undeniably back at the same time, part of me disbelieved and feared that memory. It only took a couple more moments of recall to figure out why.

I am so excited about my epiphany, I gush it all to the first person I see, my neighbor from across the street, who is several years older than me. When I'm done, I plop back on my heels in the grass, smiling, ready for her to grab my hands with delight or jump up and pirouette down the lawn. Instead, her long, mute stare cuts me, and I become afraid. "You're crazy," she slices the silence with absolute finality. And then she gets up and stalks away.

"Don't you see?" I say, "Time, death and eternity, I know how they work!" I'm standing between my chair and the dinner table, my hands stretched out, pleadingly, but my words are lost in the cacophony. Am I invisible? Suddenly, my father pauses his monologue; he noticed me! My mother's voice rushes into the vacuum left by my father's deviant calm. "Adi, don't talk crazy," she says, her tone at once dismissive and brittle. My father turns in his chair to face me, his eyes two dark drills, spinning faster and faster. "A-dri-anne," his lips and tongue carefully measure the full length of my name, his gaze holding me like a hypnotist, "You can't know that. Nobody can."

But. What. If. I. Do.

As young children, we have long discussions with invisible friends and build rockets to Mars and space stations out of plastic bricks and tubes; we watch fairies dancing in the violets, communicate silently with animals and trees, and are willing to draw a sphinx, even if we've never seen one. Adults call this "play" or "wild imaginings" and label it frivolous and immature, certainly in comparison to the important worries preoccupying *their* minds.

But, what if, at six, I actually received information I "couldn't" know? What if it was something significant, something adults didn't even imagine could be perceived? What if that is true of all children? What if each of us, walking around in adult-suits, has access to far more than we have been taught to reach for, remember, or value?

Most people's lives are peppered with the inexplicable, yet we are trained to just shrug it off: synchronicities and déjà vu, "weird" ideas that tickle the backs of our brains, impulses we can't justify, intuitions we can neither prove nor measure, passions we can't trace, insatiable curiosities that drive us, deep loves that seem to come out of nowhere.

What if that nowhere is actually some place? What if some vital part of us lives in that place? What if our early child-selves display uncanny creativity and wisdom because they are still in deep communion with those invisible, ephemeral parts of who we are?

And what if, as adults, we could have contact with that "more" of ourselves—live in an easy, natural dialogue with "unseen us," as we did when we were children? How would that change our lives, our cultures, our worlds?

I've been asking these questions since that day on Thirteenth Street when I spontaneously remembered that I used to know the answers. I haven't managed to recall all the intricacies of my suppressed childhood epiphany, but the quest that memory set me upon has been utterly life-altering. In fact, because the journey was catalyzed by such a quirky, enigmatic piece of my childhood, walking this path is not only authentically *me*, it's deeply and lastingly empowering.

Even though I do not now possess as full a grasp of the Infinite as I did at six, the winding road of remembrance has brought me potent perceptions. I see that, in the beginning, there is The One, or Source, desiring to be aware of itself. But, when you are everything, everywhere, simultaneously, how do you self-reflect? How do you...evolve? So The One diversified, creating the only thing it could: more of itself, fractals of its own consciousness.

Humans are but one kind of fractal consciousness in the infinity of All That Is. We are a special type of consciousness, though—we possess the ability to forget who and what we truly are. We experience the fear that arises out of separation from Source, yet we are coded for the ecstasy of remembering our true nature; we desire the sensation of connection—we've even named it *love*. The tension produced by these opposing emotions propels us to seek, using our physical senses to explore life in form, our minds to generate preferences and ideas, and our hearts to lead us into alignment with others, and with the more of who we are. This is a deep creation dynamic, and it expands the very fabric of existence.

Our talent for forgetting and remembering is linked to the fact that each of us is one being who possesses (at least) two points of conscious awareness.

Imagine a beam of light spreading out as it gets further away from its origin. We'll call that starting point *Source*, the light represents the vibrational energy of Source and, as it travels, it creates and illuminates existence. Now picture that light passing through lenses, like those on a camera. Since the beam is broad, it can flow through multiple lenses at once; since the light is bright, an individuated ray can pass through a string of lenses in succession and still be potent and visible, though it may dim a bit from one lens to the next. Our consciousness is the product of Source energy passing through two lenses in a line: The Ethereal Self lens, which we recognize on a spectrum as instincts, gut feelings, intuition, muse, soul, embodied god/goddess; and the Material Self lens, which we know as personality, mind, or ego.

The lenses have the effect of filtering how Source energy perceives. The Ethereal Self is like a camera lens with a short focal length and high f-stop. It's closer to Source and can handle a lot of light while maintaining focus equally on many things at once, even if they are at varying distances. It has a wide view, so it can "see the bigger picture." The Material Self acts like a camera lens with a longer focal length and a low f-stop. It's really good in dim light situations and concentrates its sharpness into a small area, highlighting the details, texture, and contours of a subject while blurring everything else in the picture. The angle of view is narrow, further focusing attention on the subject at hand by cropping out anything extraneous.

Reliance on only one of these lenses may well yield an interesting or beautiful picture, but it will never represent our whole view. We need the Material Self's narrow focus, with great magnification of detail, in order to manage and fall in love with the nitty gritty of our physical existences, and we need the wide angle and long depth of field of the Ethereal Self to see and fall in love with the variety of life around us and to receive the full flow of energy from Source.

This is how we are constructed—our lenses of consciousness built to work in effortless synergy. When these lenses are in alignment, we feel fantastic. We experience our abundance and know our worth, we thrill to the bliss of vitality and unconditional appreciation, we are inspired and excited to explore and create, and we radiate love.

Misalignment of our lenses leaves us feeling cut off, scared, alone, and disempowered. We try to compensate for that loss of connection to Source by looking to relationships, jobs, and other activities to prove our worthiness. But it never quite works, at least, not for long. We can't fabricate an internal sense of value with outside things, but we can plug into the more of what we already are and live lit up from the inside!

This is the sparkly magic of early childhood. Young children haven't lost connection with their Ethereal Selves, because human society hasn't had the chance to talk them out of it. Kids don't have full capacity to navigate the physical world on their own, but they do have full ability to receive Source energy, to dream, and to believe their dreams are important and worthy of becoming manifest. They experience themselves as fully creative, and they radiate the ecstasy of being at once both cosmic and physical.

That natural joy, which we call *child-like,* is our birthright. We are Source consciousness that chose to come into the physical to experience Playground Earth, but we never meant to lose contact with where we came from.

As adults, we feel the pure happiness of a baby's smile and it lasers through our to-do lists and our mind chatter and ignites our remembrance of easy joy—but it's temporary. We are survivors of many years of training, convincing us we can't know something we weren't taught by another human, dogs and trees don't talk, and fairies are a myth.

It's as if human society gives us a cruel choice: deny the part of yourself that isn't material and you can belong or maintain your connection with the ethereal and sacrifice your place in the manifest world.

You can't be here and be whole. Nobody can.

But. What. If. We. Are.

The last time I spoke with my friend Jillian, she told me that when she was a kid she hoarded all her allowance and chore money to buy postcards and stamps. She would hand write a card to every tourism bureau she saw advertised, asking for packets of visitor information, which she hungrily consumed. A few days after our chat, she headed off in a Dodge Ram pick-up, pulling a camper filled with art and computer supplies, to journey across the USA on her own for an entire year. This is her retirement gift to herself.

My friend Simone was raised by parents who were educators and social-change makers. Her early enchantment with cars didn't seem to fit well with the family ethic, so she abandoned engines and got a degree in psychology. After an unsatisfying stint as a counselor, she decided to go back to college; this time, though, she'd follow her rogue passion and study to be a mechanic. Since she already had a B.A., she was unable to receive financial aid for an associate degree, so she never went to automotive school. That was thirty years ago, but when I told her I was musing about quirky childhood fascinations, this story sprang immediately to mind, and I could hear regret ring in her voice.

Childhood passions deserve to be recalled, cherished, pursued. They are vital breadcrumbs on our paths to remembering our wholeness. They are place markers, energy vortices, signposts, treasure chests, genie lamps.

In my own life, I can see my youthful, deep bonding with pets leading to my work as an animal communicator, the many hours I spent ceremonially stirring buds and leaves and dirt into big pots of water heralding my practices of herbalism and sacred Goddess mysteries, and the "time, death and eternity" moment presaging my ability to read energy fields and channel guidance for people from their Ethereal Realms.

But I walked very indirect routes along the way, mired in forgetting and censure and fear. I frequently felt conflicted and riddled with self-doubt. Sometimes trauma wiped all human options away, gifting me the invitation to believe again in my Ethereal Self; sometimes its low, insistent voice persuaded me into new directions. Luckily, my early love of writing, dance, and all things art 'n crafty granted me socially acceptable avenues of access to the Ethereal, after my direct contact was repudiated and I blocked it out. I've come to appreciate that all art forms, especially non-commercial, amateur, "unskilled" endeavors, possess the capacity to bring us into connection with Source. That's why making art so often feels like love.

We all long for wholeness and authenticity. We deserve to experience abundance, ecstasy, and easy joy. We want to express the fullness of ourselves and have that touch the lives of others in positive ways. We need open, active connection with our higher octaves to do that.

The good news is, our Ethereal Self is permanently focused on the wide-angle view and always bathing us in the unconditional love that is Source. No matter who or what in the human world turns away from us, we can never actually be rejected; we are held in, we are made of, that beam of love, and we just have to relearn how to attune with it.

The truth of who and what we are is here, walking right alongside us down the street, holding hands with our inner child, waiting for us to remember.

So, what does any of this have to do with elephants?

An elephant herd's survival is attributed to what science deems the uncanny recall ability of its leader, the oldest female. Her confident responses to danger and stress indicate vast internal resources. Not only does she track the movements of every member of her own group, up to seventy individuals, she can recognize outsiders, both friends and foes, no matter how briefly or how long ago she met them. Apparently indelible inner maps of all terrain she has ever traversed enable her to guide her charges to far distant areas of water and food in times of local drought and famine.

But the influence of the matriarch elephant's mysterious powers does not end with her own herd. Elephants are a "keystone" species: their presence creates and maintains entire ecosystems, making life possible for a huge variety of fauna and flora. Without elephants, those ecosystems would fail.

It's time, beautifully human Fractal of The One,
to claim your "elephant memories."

Adrianne SpiralLight knows You are a Gift! Her offerings support and expand your inherent resonance with this Divine Truth: there is Unlimited Empowerment and Beauty in claiming your Uniqueness and Sharing it with the World. All of her work is structured to enhance your ability to connect with your Essence and foster its Blooming in your Life.

Warmth, depth and exuberance are the hallmarks of her style, whether she is translating nuanced, etheric vibration into words in a SoulBody Reading™, guiding students on wild and delight-filled journeys of self-discovery through creativity, ritual and pilgrimage, leading Spiral Write™ groups (for writers and non-writers,) or assisting individuals and businesses to flow their Highest Purpose within a matrix of grounded Abundant Exchange. Her art, writing, and photography are encoded with love to catalyze, uplift, encourage and inspire All on the Spiral Path of Embodiment of their Full and True Self.

Adrianne weaves together over 25 years of simultaneous practice as an energy intuitive and channel, animal communicator, multi-disciplinary artist, financial professional and entrepreneur. Like all humans, her main credentials are her soul blueprint and the examined depth of her life experience; in addition, she is a Reiki Master, a Master-Teacher of Essential Energy Balancing, a Certified Intentional Creativity® Teacher and Guild Member, a Priestess Initiate in the 13 Moon Mystery School, a member of the National Association of Tax Professionals, a published writer, a lay herbalist, and an award-winning photographer and fiber artist. She lives in the NYC Metro area with a beautiful and evolving ensemble of Beloveds of all species and forms.

Connect with her: SpiralLightStudios@gmail.com, AdrianneSpiralLight on FB, @adriannespirallight on IG, and **www.SpiralLightStudios.com**.

Unleash Your Essence and
Claim the Power to Create Your Life

Special Gift

SOULBODY READING

Eager to make contact with your Ethereal Self, guides and other Beings serving Your Highest Good? Want to know the state of your, or your business', energetic system—where there may be constrictions of flow and where and how to step into opportunities for expansion into your Full, True Self? Would you like to anchor in energy and awareness upgrades, specifically created for you by your Ethereal Self, to evolve your embodied ascension?

Email **SpiralLightStudios@gmail.com** with the code "ElephantMemories" to receive a special coupon for 20% off your first SoulBody Reading or Ascension Business Consultation with Adrianne.

"Changing Woman: Anchoring the Possible"
by Adrianne SpiralLight, 18 x 24, acrylic and glitter on canvas, Mabon 2018

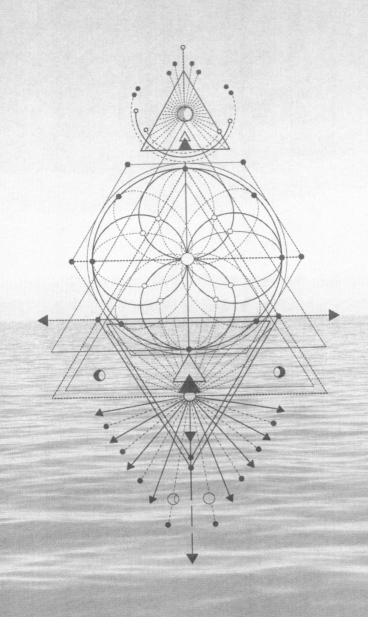

System Overload: Rebooting the Infinite Cosmos that Exists Within

BY MARY TAN

It was 2006 when the whole world collapsed in on me. I was in my Saturn's return at twenty-nine years old, and life was splitting at the seams. I couldn't stop crying long enough to sit in class. My face had a huge double bacterial infection from ear to ear that required weeks of isolated quarantine. One night, I found myself escaping death for the eighth time as I sobered up in jail for driving under the influence. Numbing the pain of existence was the main coping mechanism I had to survive the past few decades. Lacking the tools to navigate an empowered life, I attempted suicide at nineteen. I am grateful to still be here. Ultimately, it was the crushing weight of rape, abortion, abandonment, and childhood abuse that broke the beautiful spirit of a young lady who believed the only escape route was death.

I was on system overload.

Without an anchor to keep me grounded into this life, I felt like a flag being torn to shreds by a fierce tornado. I felt like a bottle of soda that has been shaken a hundred times, then left in the sun to bake in the summer sun.

The pressure built up and exploded my dark mortifying pain onto everything around me. Decades of suppressed emotions, as a way to gain love, acceptance, and belonging, came spewing out all at once. No longer was I able to hold it together or contain the toxicity of unprocessed trauma within my being. All systems had reached their overload capacity, and now I was left with the aftermath of a life malfunction that looked like a nuclear plant meltdown, all alarms ringing. Without an iota of reference for what just happened, I was brought to my knees begging the Divine for mercy.

Can someone...anyone...please help me?!

All I could think of was how I wished I knew what was wrong with me because maybe then I could fix it. After all, I was left without adult supervision since the age of thirteen, so I was a natural problem-solver and a resourceful survivor. But crying for 365 days straight frightened the hell out of me. Was I losing my mind and going crazy? Just before the mental breakdown, I had earned a psychology degree from New York University and moved to San Diego to study Chinese Medicine. I was intuitively following my interests and started experimenting with veganism, meditation, chanting, and feng shui. I was wide open, desperately soul searching, seeking, looking for myself somewhere out there in the Universe. It was a lonely road, and I felt utterly lost, without a rudder, abandoned in the middle of the ocean. "God," I often called out. "Are you there? Why am I here? What am I doing here?"

In hindsight, what felt like the darkest nights of my soul served as the beginning of the end. Only through closing one cycle could the next evolution begin. Although it was one of the toughest times of my life, it was also the answer to my prayers. Letting the old matrix within me die made space for the rebirth of a new world. Every one of my beliefs had to pass through its judgment day to be rendered relevant or irrelevant in my new paradigm.

As children, we learn how to navigate this big scary world from the elders around us, but what if what they were taught was distorted and untrue? What would happen if I detached from the familiar yet false sense of safety, created by the ropes of life, handed down to me from birth? Is their version of success true for me? What if there was a better way? A way that I could feel out and discover through curiosity, intuition, creativity, and love. It took massive courage to carve out my own path and live life to the highest degree. I had to journey into the hidden chambers deep within myself to discover the freedom that comes from knowing my true self. This is blissful liberation.

There is a whole new world waiting to be discovered within your own being. Would you be willing to go there, Divine One? There within lies the true path to Heaven. Come with me beloved, I want to show you a way to ascend out of the muck and into the light. You will remember as we go along, for there is nothing to teach or learn—simply the remembrance of what you've always known.

I believe that before this incarnation you sat with your masters, teachers, and loved ones to review past lessons and design your upcoming life for the sake of expanding your awareness and consciousness, so that you can have new experiences through the physical form. As the pure spiritual self begins its transition into physical form, it enters with past lessons to revisit and new lessons chosen for its evolution. At the moment of conception, when the sperm meets the egg, the mother vessel's DNA, beliefs, vibration, frequency, cellular memory, limiting programs, and undigested traumas rush into the zygote all at once. Imprinted with that particular blueprint for life, the child gestates through the months hearing, feeling, sensing, and knowing all that the mother is experiencing, further confirming the map it was given. Absolutely everything impacts this new life, including the father's mindset, environmental factors, relationships with others, food, drink, air quality, and more.

Here's a real client example. Shelly's parents were already in an unhealthy relationship when her mother became pregnant. When I took her back to the moment of conception, all she could hear was her mother's fear-ridden thoughts thinking "I don't want this child" over and over again. Understandably, her mother didn't want to raise a child in a rocky environment. Even with good intentions, a deep sense of rejection, being unlovable, and not belonging imprinted the zygote-self right then and there as her life operating system. This imprint emits a frequency like a homing device, attracting more of that same vibrational experience to appear in different manifestations. No amount of running and hiding can make it go away.

The great news is, these disempowering blueprints can be removed and healed so anyone can evolve into an empowered life. Once a child is born into the world, she is taught how to perceive the world, how to be in it, how to fit in, be loved, accepted, succeed, survive, and keep the cycle of life going according to tradition, habit, or decree. What if those ways came from a fear of losing love, rather than moving toward love as an inspiration? What would it look like to break free from outdated ways and shed all attachments in order to float with the natural essence of life's love, also known as bliss? What if the world, as a whole, was largely asleep and trapped in an illusion that seems unmistakably real? You, me, us...we all came for one purpose: to remember who we really are. You are the Divine light who has chosen to come forth at this time to wake yourself up from the nightmare of separation and reunite with the Source within you as the driver of your body vehicle and mind. Once you have shaken yourself up to a sobered state, you must cultivate daily practices to stay activated as the clear lighthouse in a storm. These daily practices are non-negotiable, or else the ego-self will undermine your evolution at the weakest link. It wants to preserve its existence by stopping you from the ultimate goal of allowing the spirit-self to drive your being. Rather than vilify the ego-self, let us recognize its purpose, strengths, and weaknesses and then repeatedly choose to put it in its place as a follower not the leader—a servant to your Divine self.

You are a soul here to lead the body through partnership. The spirit-self is an emanation of the Most High: the Divine, the ineffable, unnamable intelligence that breathes life into all things. As humans, we must admit that we know a fraction of a fraction of the whole concept of existence. The intricacies of this grand intelligence are infinite and ever-expanding. We have no way of knowing all from our limited, singular perspective. Most humans get caught in a cycle where the brain tells them what to think, which instantly informs how they feel, what actions they take, and the resulting effects that follow. However, once you remember your powerful role, turn that around and let your soul tell the brain what to think so that the whole chain of events may now serve the highest good with ease and grace.

You want an abundant flow of wealth, love, health, balance, harmony, collaboration, joy, community, and bliss? You can have it! The way there is by entering into the sacred chamber of your heart during quiet meditation with the intention of meeting your inner being, the Divine, God, the Universe, the Source, and the infinite well of life force energy. Did you know that you are an eternal, infinite extension of love?

The heart as a portal of ascension has always been there—the channel of connection is unbreakable and the flow of love is inexhaustible.

To access its gifts to the highest degree, it requires your participation, continuous focus, and directed efforts in perceptions, attitudes, beliefs, thoughts, words, deeds, actions, and choices. You have free will and choice, therefore, you have ultimate control in the out-picturing of the movie you live out in each incarnation. The external unfolding of your life is a projection from your internal universe. You and this internal universe are also part of the whole universe. Every little thing has meaning, and every tiny piece is related to the next. We are in an ever-expanding cycle of evolution to remember who we are as a collective race. The moment we all wake up from the dream is the moment earth and its people ascend to the next level of conscious awareness.

The daily dramas and stories that trap you into complaining, retaliating, or harboring resentments are the ego-self playing on your pain points to smoke screen you from attaining the true goal of your life: to evolve out of the stories in order to remember your Divine light and shine so brightly you awaken all those around you. The path to shining bright evokes limiting beliefs—that are eons old—of why it is unsafe, unkind, and undesirable to do so. These limiting beliefs cause most people to pull back rather than shine.

The challenges in the game of life at earth school are multi-leveled. You, as a mighty, powerful being, however, thought it would be fun to roam the earth and included many signposts and mile markers to encourage yourself along the way. It's like coming to a foreign planet with your eyes blindfolded, ears plugged, and GPS thrown out the window as you scavenger hunt for the holy grail. Each round is timed by the average human lifespan, and there are so many artificial rules that are not in alignment with ultimate Truth that your computation system goes haywire! You doubt yourself completely and wish to abort this life mission...except, it's too late. You just got here. Good luck and GO! Hahaha. The good news is, you do have an internal GPS called intuition, and all your true senses of inner sight, hearing, and knowing are intact within you. All you have to do is flip on the control panel, activate power, and drive your ship to the Light.

To make the game even more interesting, each incarnation is impacted by the lessons unlearned from past lives, current life programming, and karmic effects from your ancestral lineage. Your ancestral lineage refers to your own mother and father lines going back to the beginning of time. They all had lessons, of course. Since your soul is energy and energy never dies, it continuously transforms as you incarnate through infinite lifetimes, learning and expanding.

The collective consciousness is the collection of every human's conscious and unconscious beliefs, stored in what I like to describe as an iCloud—an energetic storage space of all the beliefs that humans subscribe to, as a collective. All the unbelievably dark events airing out on the global scene at this time are the unprocessed wounds of the human race. As these wounds rise to the top to be detoxed, healed, and released, they make way for a new matrix to anchor onto the planet. This new paradigm is the wish granted for a world operating from love, collaboration, abundance, harmony, and joy. It is a response to the billions of prayers asking for something better than all the pain and hurt surfacing to the top right now. Without the negativity rising, the prayers would not have come so intently at such a high rate at the same time. It is this focused energy with heightened emotion and a clear call to the universe that the law of attraction is responding to. Hence, everything serves a purpose; even the most atrocious acts on the planet can lead us back to love.

I was forty years old when my conscious mind accepted the memory of childhood sexual trauma from the depths of my subconscious mind. The brain will hide things from you to sidestep a mental breakdown. I did not want to see that memory, but I found the courage to push myself because I knew it had multiple levels of healing for myself, my children, past generations, the future, and the collective consciousness. What is done for one, is done for all. When you heal your internal files of victimization, you heal it for the whole of humanity. Every time someone has the bravery to go where no one wants to go, look at the ugliest parts of what we're capable of experiencing or perpetrating, and transmute it alchemically, you are literally wiping it out from the human condition one file, one pixel, one story at a time. And that is the spiritual movement that we are in. We are alive in very impactful times as we awaken to the Truth of why we exist, why we are here, what we are meant to do, and remember the Divinity of our sovereign selves.

You are a Divine Human. You exist as a soul within a physical vehicle. The journey is to shed the layers of illusion over and over again until you are left with only the purity of your Light. The way to undo the stories, blue-prints, and imprints is to practice deep self-awareness, cultivate self-knowl-edge, and stay in constant contact with the true self within. Remember that the external reality is much like a dream state where you must wake yourself up repeatedly! Remain consciously connected to the infinite intelligence at all times and trust the journey. Eventually, you will be able to lead others to awaken with you to co-create a world that flourishes with love, abundance, collaboration, joy, and harmony.

This blissful heaven exists now.

Entry is attained by an elevated frequency through dedicated conscious evo-lution on a personal level. When you heal yourself, you actually heal the world. The parts are in the whole and the whole is in the parts—As Above, So Below.

So are you ready to take that leap out of system overload and into the infinite cosmos that exists within you? You inspire me with your courage! I see you; I honor you; I thank you. You are not alone on the path. Keep shining bright!

Mary Tan is an international bestselling author, thought leader and speaker who teaches people how to shed the painful struggles of life and activate the Universal flow for clarity, confidence and joy to fill your life. Humanity is evolving consciously at a rapid pace. She shows you how to navigate this new terrain with empowered presence. Mary is a sought-after expert for radio, podcasts, magazines, and shows around the world. When not having fun sharing the stage with Deepak Chopra and Les Brown, you can find Mary teaching metaphysics to the kids at the school she founded called, the Light Warrior School. Mary is on Facebook and Instagram **@marytanempowers.** Email her at **mary@marytanempowers.**

Special Gift

THE KEYS OF ASCENSION

While your personal story might be different, there are common threads that connect us all right now as we trek through this current phase of humanity's conscious evolution. Things are breaking down. What once worked, no longer works. What once made sense, no longer makes sense! It can be downright terrifying sometimes. Believe me, I totally get it! What I've found is this breakdown is the lead-up to our collective breakthrough. And you, light leader, are on the front lines carving out a new path for us all. Ready to get some support on navigating this uncharted territory? I've created this gift just for leaders like you who are here to spread the light and guide the way. You can get your copy at **www.thekeysofascension.com.** Thank you for hearing the call, taking action, and being the example that inspires others onto the path. Together we have strength in numbers, synergy, and positive change. You are so loved!

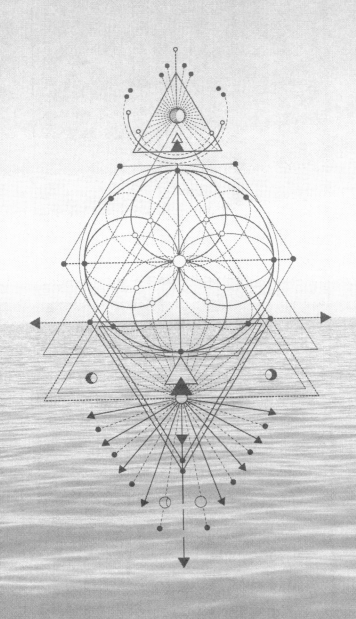

A Beautiful Mess

BY LARA WYNN

"You bitch! You fucking slut!" she yelled, lunging at me. "You've ruined my family and my marriage!"

He blocked her, grabbed her hand, and put himself in front of me so she couldn't hurt me. She was surprisingly agile and fast for someone supposedly in the final stages of cancer. He had lied to me about that, too.

The damage was already done. Those words coming out of the mouth of another woman stung and shook me to my core. The irony was not lost on me that we were in the parking lot of a big community art and healing festival celebrating "love."

How could I have gotten to such a low place and made these choices that had harmed others?

I had been in need of more tenderness, affection, and physical, sensual touch so it made sense that we ended up together. He was one of the first men in my life who appreciated my life experience and did not treat me condescendingly or discourage me from my full sexual expression.

However, what I didn't realize at the time was that he was attracted to my energy and fed off of it. I was open, confident, and liberated. He lived his life in fear and was afraid to be honest about his feelings and needs. So he drowned his feelings and swallowed away his needs with alcohol and sexual encounters outside of his marriage.

The intimate details, like the fact that I was in an open marriage, and how I chose to get myself into this mess, don't really matter. What does matter is that I engaged in harmful, dishonest behavior. I deeply regret this and for years, carried shame about this part of my life and my not-so-healthy choices. But now, I am able to choose self-compassion rather than beating myself up with self-inflicted moralistic judgments.

In this particular nightmare, I realized that I had attracted yet again another codependent person into my life. The time had come for this pattern in my life to end because I was *done* with this drama! I decided right then and there that I would never again engage in negative and harmful behavior just to get *my* needs met. I made a conscious choice to operate from a higher-level question: *Before I take this action or enter into a relationship, is this for the highest benefit of all?* My desire to change does not come out of shame, guilt, anger or depression, but from a genuine desire to contribute to the well-being of ALL life—including my own.

With a pained expression on his face, he looked at me, then back at her, then back at me again and said, "You and I can no longer be around each other or contact each other ever again."

I couldn't believe this was happening—it felt like a horribly bad dream that I couldn't wake myself up from. After a pause, I said, "Okay," and walked away from my dear friend of nine years turned lover those past two years.

I walked up the steps and entered the festival venue in a daze. Everyone was so joyful, music was playing, and people were dancing and celebrating our wonderful community. I don't remember taking the elevator to the upper floor to be in the "quiet resting room"...I think I was in shock. Somehow, that is where I ended up, plopped down on a soft comfy cushion in the quiet meditation room—the same room I had just spent hours decorating the day before for this event. I curled up in the fetal position and covered myself with a blanket as tears rolled down my cheeks and my body began to shake uncontrollably at the violence and loss I had just experienced.

Suddenly my phone rang and brought me back to the present. Was it him calling? Or her? Does it matter now? Do I answer it? It was made very clear that we were not to contact each other ever again. Maybe she was "testing" me to see if I was lying. I decided not to answer it. I put my phone on silent. It vibrated that I had a voicemail. I put the phone down and sat up. I closed my eyes and put my hand over my heart as I slowed down my breath and attempted to feel some sort of connection to myself. After several minutes I felt calmer as my breath returned to its normal rate. I looked down at the phone: ten missed calls and ten voicemail messages! *Did something happen to them? Did they get into a car accident? Why would he tell me never to see or have contact with him again and then immediately call me? Shit, they have young children, what if something really had happened to them? I better at least listen to the first voice message.*

Bracing myself, I pressed the voicemail message on my phone—it was him. "Lara, I'm so sorry she almost hurt you. I really need you to call me back and clear up some things for her. I need you to tell her how often and how long we were together. She doesn't believe me. Please...I won't ever ask you for anything else again. I don't want to lose my kids!" He was close to crying and she was weeping in the background. I hoped that they were pulled over somewhere and not driving during all of this.

How had I attracted this man into my life? Could it be because he was nurturing, playful, affectionate, and in need of physical nurturing touch—and I have so much love to give? In a twisted way, I had felt sorry for him and wanted him to experience the healing of sensual touch with me that he was lacking in his life.

I looked down at my phone again—he had left several text messages and voicemails. I took a deep breath and called him. "Please just tell her that it was only a few times and didn't mean anything..."

I cut him off right in the middle of his wanting to create another lie.

"No! For once I'm not going to bail you out of the mess that you created and the choices you made! If I talk to her I'm going to tell her the *whole* truth and exactly how many years this has been going on. If you love her, you will tell her the truth! You didn't just lie to her, you lied to me! If you had the courage to share your feelings and needs with her, maybe you two could have worked things out, looked into an open, ethical, non-monogamous relationship, or ended the relationship. I *begged* you to tell her the truth, to even explore the option of an open marriage, but you were too afraid and instead you ended up really hurting those around you—who you claimed to love. I regret that I was not a stronger person and didn't insist on this or end it with you. And now, you and I can't even remain friends, and I'm hurt and I'm grieving the loss of not being with you again. I know now that I was a simple way for you to relax and get a momentary high—an escape from your real feelings and needs. Look, I'm always going to love you and I really hope you get some help for yourself. Your children need you. But you don't get to blame the decisions you made on me! You knew what you were doing. I truly wish you the best in your life and I hope you find your own happiness inside. I am blocking your number! Do not contact me again—you *know* this is for the best."

I hung up.

I sighed deeply, feeling the relief of letting go and releasing all the pent-up emotion inside of me. I felt a loosening around my heart and a softening in my entire body.

For a while, I was angry and defensive about the situation. But over time, I realized that I needed to take radical responsibility for my life and really look at what had caused me to get into the situation in the first place. I needed to explore the deep internal shame I was carrying around this experience.

Up until that point in my life, I had tried to follow society's rules and expectations—go to school, get good grades, date one boy at a time, go to college, get good grades, graduate, establish your career, get married, have kids, live happily ever after, grow old together and die.

This way of life was definitely *not* modeled for me by my parents' relationship. When my dad was already married, he had an adulterous affair with my mom. When I was four years old, he left his first wife and married my mom. I was the flower girl at my own parents' wedding. Then, my mom died when I was seventeen, and my dad remarried his first wife out of guilt.

I knew something was definitely different about me. Growing up, I secretly desired to date both guys and girls—something that one *absolutely, positively* did not do in the 1980s. Career-wise, I also knew that I would *never* be happy in the public relations field, essentially lying for corporations that caused environmental disasters.

I made an unusual choice as a young adult to get married and work—while my husband finished school and established his career—have children and home-school them. This was me consciously choosing to be Suzy home-maker and put my career on hold. I chose this lifestyle as a rebellion against what society had deemed my path.

I was never a "normal" mom. I home-birthed my children and always lived a holistic lifestyle. When my first marriage ended after seventeen years, I knew that something inside of me was still stifled, and so I embraced my true sexuality and sensuality as a person who loves more than one person. My first marriage ended with me embracing what I *thought* was true freedom.

But I was actually repeating a similar pattern—I was looking outside of myself for validation by jumping into another relationship with a man—one who in private accepted my true sexuality and agreed to an open relationship. But several years into the marriage he revealed that he had only agreed to it because he didn't want to lose me.

My need to be accepted was so strong that I had ignored all of the red flags about this current relationship until it was too late—and I ended up in this mess where I had hurt another woman through my own selfishness.

I now know that I was dealing with an old wound...the belief that "*just being me*" causes disaster and harm. And I perpetuated this belief by finding myself in a relationship where my true self was not acceptable.

As I look back, I can see the gifts in this whole experience. It's awakened me to my shadow side and shown me the deeply ingrained belief that if I was to be my true loving and authentic self, I would somehow sabotage myself and my relationships, or hurt someone.

Now I know deep in my being that I can clear the lower vibrations, heal the shame, and still have my needs met—without anyone getting hurt. I am aware of my old patterns and the energy I was putting out that was attracting codependent partners. And, as an adult child of an alcoholic, I've learned to be extremely conscious and mindful of my role in those dynamics.

The process of writing about this experience of healing and finding self-forgiveness has given me great insight. Being vulnerable and sharing my story—no matter how shameful it feels—allows me to release hidden threads of shame and guilt and replace them with self-love. I've learned that shame holds us back from fully living and enjoying life. Holding on to guilt and operating from that place can manifest into illness and poor health. It can quite literally eat you up inside and even kill you.

It has been quite a journey coming home to my authentic self and releasing the need for external validation. I no longer need people to like or approve of me.

I chose to forgive myself and embarked on an extreme self-love journey to experience a deep connection to my truth. To accomplish this, I made my primary relationship the one with *myself*. I immersed myself in meditation, ecstatic dance, authentic Tantra practices, and learning about nonviolent communication.

Ecstatic dance has been a wonderful tool for releasing the need for others to validate me. It has helped me release stored traumas in my body without having to dwell in the story of them. There is actually no need for me to relive the trauma anymore, instead I am focused on releasing it and letting it go. Animals in the wild constantly experience high-stress states, yet they don't go see Dr. Elephant and tell them about the narrow escape from the lion that was preying on them for dinner!

The ecstatic dance communities I have been a part of, such as the amazing Dance Your Soul™ community (www.danceyoursoul.net), have provided a safe space for me to allow whatever stress or trauma I'm holding in my body to move through and be released. I allow myself to feel any trapped pain, fear, sadness, anger, overwhelm, or anxiety, and then witness it leave my energetic and physical body. I am left in a blissful and ecstatic state.

As people, we want to feel good...and yet, we feel badly when we do! I finally came into my truth around my sexuality without shame. This is not an easy thing to do with the culture and my family of origin telling me otherwise. I had to reframe my old belief, "I can only love one person," into a new and expanded belief that reflects my truth: "I love with multiple souls regardless of gender or sexual orientation. Love is love."

Pleasure allows us to connect with our authentic selves. You recognize your needs and desires and become an expert on what you are feeling, instead of the actor on the TV commercial *telling* you how you are feeling. You choose to go outside for a walk in the park instead of running to the nearest fast food place for that cheeseburger, choosing instead to feed your unmet need with the beauty of nature rather than calories. Feeding your soul instead of your stomach, which then allows you to make more aligned choices around food that not only tastes good, but is nourishing and healthy, too!

Commit to loving yourself so that you can freely love others. When you experience connection to *self*, you realize you are safe in the relationships you create, and that you do not need to rely solely on your partner or partners to meet your needs. Instead, you ask the question, "Is this action or non-action for the highest good of all?" Things become simpler. If it isn't a "Hell, yes!", then it's a "Hell, no!"

I now feel I am in alignment with my true authentic self; my radiance is shining brightly because I have seen the gift and the shadow in this experience. I continue to do the inner work. I'm human and will make mistakes as that is how we grow. I appreciate all the life lessons and growth—the good, the bad, and the ugly! It's led to me getting published and to discovering success in new ways. I now experience healthier relationships, I attract people who I love to serve, and I have a waiting list of clients who want to hire me as their Authentic Tantra Practitioner and Coach. My life's purpose and sacred work is now manifesting, because I am finally in integrity and have released the shame that was running the show behind the scenes for so long.

We are *all* healers and possess radiance, which consists of our unique magic and gifts. But when we haven't dealt with the trauma in our lives, then we will remain blocked and our radiance and gifts will not be activated. It is so worth doing the work to release your blocks and activate your gifts! I now feel more joy, not just a fleeting blissed-out moment, but one of the highest vibrations that gently guides me into deeper intimacy with my own heart. I now listen with my heart and feel alive and in the flow of joy and love. This, to me, is true freedom.

Life is a beautiful mess, and it's yours to embrace. I desire that you, too experience the freedom of being who you really are! This is why I have shared my story with you, to inspire you to live in alignment with your truest self and experience the feeling of liberation and sovereignty that await you.

Lara Wynn, Evocateur and Founder of the Heart of Living Fully Program, is a Soulistic Wellness and Ecstatic Life Coach who brings over twenty years of life and professional experience to her clients. Bringing together her natural curiosity and passion for life, Lara is a multi-passionate entrepreneur with an extensive background. She holds a B.A. in Communication Studies, is  a Licensed Massage Therapist, Certified Holistic Health Coach, Yoga Instructor, Tony Robbins Business Mastery graduate, and is currently pursuing her certification in Authentic Tantra through the Institute of Authentic Tantra Education. She is also a doTERRA essential oil Wellness Advocate, co-creator of life (aka mom), partner, lover, Firewalker, writer, volunteer, peace promoter, and bliss-spreader.

Seeing service as a portal to self-love, Lara enjoys giving back to her community and serves as the Administrative Coordinator for the Big Love Network—a non-profit organization dedicated to building bridges and sparking creative collaborations across socioeconomic and cultural barriers. The core of the network consists of organizers, permaculturists, healing practitioners, and artists who facilitate neighbor-led, creative peacemaking, sustainability, and health equity efforts throughout Akron, Ohio as a means for social change.

Lara is tuned in, tapped in, and turned on to the Universe and loves to create experiences where people feel alive, in the flow, and joyful. She uses various healing tools, modalities, her connection to Source, and her intuition to support her clients in celebrating life through embodied movement practices such as ecstatic dance, healing meditations, and her special Evoke essential oil blends that support each person's unique health and life goals. Learn more at **www.LaraWynn.com.**

Special Gift

FREE PLEASURE GUIDE WITH
JOURNALING INSTRUCTIONS

"Pleasure: A Healing Guide for the Heart of Living Fully."

This guide will help you experience more pleasure in all areas of your life, offering tools that help you recognize and meet your pleasure needs. Remembering this intimate inner knowledge will foster a deeper connection to your true Self.

Access here: **www.larawynn.com/setsail**

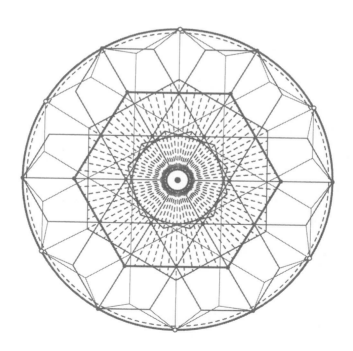

FLOWER OF LIFE PRESS BOOKS

The New Feminine Evolutionary: Embody Presence—Become the Change

Pioneering the Path to Prosperity: Discover the Power of True Wealth and Abundance

Sacred Body Wisdom: Igniting the Flame of Our Divine Humanity

Practice: Wisdom from the Downward Dog

Emerge: 7 Steps to Transformation (No matter what life throws at you!)

Sisterhood of the Mindful Goddess: How to Remove Obstacles, Activate Your Gifts, and Become Your Own Superhero

Path of the Priestess: Discover Your Divine Purpose

Sacred Call of the Ancient Priestess: Birthing a New Feminine Archetype

Rise Above: Free Your Mind One Brushstroke at a Time

Menopause Mavens: Master the Mystery of Menopause

The Power of Essential Oils: Create Positive Transformation in Your Well-Being, Business, and Life

Self-Made Wellionaire: Get Off Your Ass(et), Reclaim Your Health, and Feel Like a Million Bucks

Oms From the Mat: Breathe, Move, and Awaken to the Power of Yoga

Oms From the Heart: Open Your Heart to the Power of Yoga

The Four Tenets of Love: Open, Activate, and Inspire Your Life's Path

The Fire-Driven Life: Ignite the Fire of Self-Worth, Health, and Happiness with a Plant-Based Diet

Becoming Enough: A Heroine's Journey to the Already Perfect Self

The Caregiving Journey: Information. Guidance. Inspiration.

Visit us at **www.FlowerofLifepress.com**

Made in the USA
Lexington, KY
24 October 2019